MW00719880

GOLD BUCKLE DREAMS

GOLD BUCKLE DREAMS

The Rodeo Life
of
Chris LeDoux

by
David G. Brown

WOLVERINE GALLERY
Basin

The cover. Chris LeDoux ''Marking out'' on Steiner's Stormy Weather as the bronc makes his high dive. This was Chris' tenth and final ride at the 1976 National Finals Rodeo, in Oklahoma City, Oklahoma. Chris and Stormy Weather collected seventy-eight points on this ride which won him the 1976 Bareback Championship of the World.

Copyright © 1986 by David G. Brown
All rights reserved, including the right of reproduction in whole or in part in any form. First Wolverine printing 1989.

Library of Congress Cataloging-in-Publication Data.
Brown, David G., 1957—
Gold Buckle Dreams
1. LeDoux, Chris. 2. Cowboys-United States-Biography. 3. Composers-United States-Biography. 4. Rodeos-United States. I. Title.
GV1833.6.L43B76 1987 791'.8 [B] 86-43250
ISBN: 0-941875-08-3 (pbk.)

First published: Boston, Quinlan, 1987

Printed in the United States of America

4 5 6 7 8 9 10

Published by Wolverine Gallery
P. O. Box 24
Basin, WY 82410

Printed by Pioneer Printing
P.O. Box 466
Cheyenne, Wyoming 82003-0466

Foreword

Bucking horses can kill ya. They can cripple you for life. They can make an old man out of you before your time. They'll splatter you against the back of the chute. They'll stick your head in the dirt. They'll drag you around the arena, hung-up, and walk all over you. At the very least they'll keep your riding arm sore until you decide to hang it up for good.

You'll spend countless hours driving all night, choking down rank black coffee to keep you awake so you can get to the next rodeo, just to let another bronc give your body more abuse.

You'll sleep in the truck and eat cold beans out of a can, so you can buy gas and pay your entry fees at another rodeo ... hoping you can win a couple of hundred bucks so you can buy more gas and pay more fees and take more punishment.

You'll draw sorry horses no one has ever won a nickle on. You'll draw the rank ones that will rip your hand out of the riggin' and throw you out the back end.

Then, on that special day, you may be at Cheyenne or the Podunk County Fair, and it may be pouring down rain or 110 degrees in the shade, but everything clicks. You draw that good one.

Your confidence is at a peak. You nod your head and it all comes together. The horse blows in the air, you get tapped. You feel the power under you and in your own body. You are right on the ragged edge, taking it to the limit, making that wild ride. The whistle blows.

You get off and walk back to the chutes. The crowd is going wild and your friends shake your hand and slap you on the back and say, "Good ride, cowboy."

This is what makes all the tough times worth while.

The warm feeling you get after that good ride is worth more than all the prize money or the silver-mounted saddles or the trophy belt-buckles you'll ever win . . . except maybe for one . . . the big gold one that says, "PRCA World's Champion."

Chris LeDoux

This book is dedicated to the cowboys and cowgirls of the Professional Rodeo Cowboys Association. Their courage and determination have made Rodeo America's number-one sport.

Special thanks to the ProRodeo Hall of Champions in Colorado Springs, Colorado, for its assistance and guidance.

Thanks to Andrea Aldridge for her work on the manuscript.

This road that I've chosen, it's a road that few have traveled,
But there's good times with the hard times along the way.
And this life that I'm living, God knows that I love it,
And I'd like to share it with you, if I may.

So I write my songs of life as I know it,
And I sing them for everyone to hear.
And in my songs, I hope, you'll understand just a little
What it's like to be a Rodeo Man.

> —Chris LeDoux, from the introduction to
> the album *Life as a Rodeo Man* (Wyoming
> Brand Music)

Introduction

Cowboys were not meant to be different, they just are. They didn't want to be special, but in many people's eyes, they just are, whether it be Chris LeDoux, Casey Tibbs, Larry Mahan, Jim Shoulders, or any of the great, great forgotten heroes of the rodeo world and Western fame.

I, too, always wanted to be a champion, a "Gold Buckle cowboy." But God blessed me with the brains to realize I was not going to be that champion. I also realized that if I wanted the lifestyle described in books like this and in lives like these, I could have it—by talking about it.

On the Great American Cowboy™ radio network, and a few other places, I've been proud to talk of a man known as "The Great American Cowboy." Tall crowned hats and high-heeled boots and the way of the western man riding off into the sunset ... tight jeans and a string with a Bull Durham tab hanging out of his pocket, and a handkerchief with the tip hanging off the side ... put a gold buckle on his belt and you are inviting the greatest gusto that God ever put in a man. *That* makes him different, makes him the way he likes to be—it's called "balance."

Some people call them athletes, some people call them cowboys, and some people call them coyotes, but they're born to be professionals. From behind that buckle they walk with a different presence, a majestic manner of motion that makes them totally different from every other breed of man or woman. And they do it with a grin!

It's not the size of the buckle on his belt that makes the cowboy. It's not how much fight there is in the man that makes him the champion. It's not how much buck there is in the horse that makes him so good. It's the spirit that they're born with. You'll not find this spirit any stronger in any man than Chris LeDoux.

I've known many men like Chris LeDoux who have come so close to peak perfection: in their sport or their event, or in their lives. They understand what the Lord has given them. He creates within them a special "try" and that special "balance." You'll find as you read this book that cowboys are, indeed, "different."

David Brown has captured some phenomenal, literally phenomenal, ideas within men, women, their families and their lifestyles. As you read this book, you'll find a different reason for a gold buckle on every page. I hope that you'll read it as easily as it is written for you to read, and enjoy it, savoring it like a good, fire-cooked steak.

I'm proud to be a cowboy, and I'm proud to be a part of this literature. Whether Chris LeDoux, Jim Shoulders, Larry Mahan, or myself, nothing makes us any prouder than to be called "one of the Great American Cowboys."

Happy Trails!

Bob Tallman

Chapter 1

The Winner

When he was a boy and dreamed of being a man,
Prob'ly dreamed everything that a young boy can.
He's a lover, a fighter and a saddlebronc rider—
An all-around hell of a hand.
Well, the chutes are all loaded, the riggin's are set,
Lord, the cowboys are ready to ride.
He's pulled down his hat, and he's spit out his chew,
Be a hot time in the old town tonight.

The horse in chute eight, he's a-kickin' the gate.
Lord, he's big and he's hard and he's crazy.
And the chute boss is hollerin', "Come on, boys, get on 'em,
I'm commencin' to think you're all lazy."
With his spurs in his shoulders, the horse comes unglued.
It's like riding some kind of explosion.
And the bronc, he starts spinnin', the cowboy's a-grinnin',
Doin' fine there in all the commotion.

The crowd's on its feet, and the whistle, she blows,
The pick-up men rush to his side.
As they pull him away, he hears one of them say,
"Looks to me like a winning ride."
And the spotlight's on the sawdust that shines in his brain,
And his dreams are the bones in his soul.
And it's all comin' true, right in front of his eyes,
'Cause he's the cowboy who won the big rodeo.

Gary McMahan (Yodeling Yahoo Music),
from **Rodeo and Living Free**

"Put me down for one of them bulls," the young cowboy demanded proudly.

Tommy Steiner chuckled at the prospect of this tenderfoot climbing onto one of his practice bulls, but the stock contractor picked a short Charolais bull with stubby horns and pointed him out to the eager cowboy.

Without hesitation, Chris LeDoux climbed up onto the chute and began rigging up the beast for his ride. The braided rope, with a bell tied into a loop at one end and a woven handle a few feet from the other end, was slipped around the bull and left to hang loosely. Cecil Hill, owner of the arena and host for the practice riding, and several veteran cowboys gathered around to lend a hand and offer advice to the novice rider.

With the arena cleared and the flank strap in place, Chris put on his freshly rosined glove, secured it to his wrist with a leather thong, then slipped onto the Charolais's back. He began warming up the tail of his rope, as he had seen it done a hundred times before, by dusting some rosin onto the rope, then grasping it firmly with his gloved hand and briskly sliding it up and down the rope. The friction heated the rosin, melting it into the rope and glove to make both very sticky. Then he turned the tail over to Hill, who had climbed up on the chute gate and was now leaning into the chute to help Chris. The twelve-year-old pushed his gloved hand into the braided handle and with his free hand adjusted the loose rope to the center of the bull's back. As soon as Chris was sure the rope was placed just right, Hill began pulling it up tight.

"Now you let me know when it's tight enough, Chris," he said.

". . . That's good," Chris muttered, taking the tail from Cecil and laying it across the palm of his riding hand, on top of the handle, then wrapping it firmly behind and around his wrist as he closed his hand into a tight fist, clutching the handle and the tail. With his free right hand he pulled down his big hat and looked at Hill one last time.

"Now look," the weathered old cowboy began, "if you feel yourself going to one side, just go ahead and get off. Don't try to hang on, 'cause you'll get hurt."

With that, Chris nodded his head for the gate—on his very first bull ride.

Almost from the first jump he felt himself slipping to one side. Remembering the advice Cecil had given him, he jerked himself free and leaped to safety. As he brushed himself off, he was greeted by the group of broadly smiling cowboys, who patted him on the back, laughing at his short ride.

Misunderstanding their laughter, Chris's feelings were hurt. He was more than a little disappointed in himself for coming off so quickly, but he tried to hide his feelings with a weak smile. Shuffling his feet nervously, he quickly pulled away from the group to go retrieve his bull rope from the arena. Hill noticed the boy's disappointment and walked out into the arena to talk with him in private.

"Chris, you did a mighty fine job, for your first time out," he began.

"Yeah, but everyone's laughing at me back there," Chris replied sorely.

"You gotta learn something real quick, Chris. These boys have all been right where you are today. Behind these chutes they will laugh—and laugh *with* you, not *at* you. They've earned that right, because they, too, have looked down on those horns.

"Now, out there," Cecil pointed towards the nearly empty bleachers, "those folks don't have a thing to say. They've never been in here. It takes guts to do what you did today, and it will take more guts to keep gettin' on 'em. But I figure you're a tryer, and we'll see you on 'em again."

Chris pushed at a pebble with his boot toe as a grin began to play across his face. Cecil continued, "I could tell the minute you hit the dirt you were hooked. You know why?"

Chris shook his head.

"Because when you hit the dirt, you rolled over, and through the dust and dirt we could all see that big old Texas grin. I've seen a bunch of young punchers set down on their first head, and they'll either come up with a look of sheer terror on their faces, in which case they'll never do it again, or a silly grin, like yours. You're hooked, boy, and all these guys back here are, too. They know you've caught the bug, and by showing the courage to get down on one, you've passed your initiation. You're one of them now, part of the club. Now get back over there and take your hazing. You'll have lots of chances to poke fun at newcomers to the club as you go along, but now it's your turn to take the licks with a grin.''

By the time he finished talking, Chris's face had begun to beam with pride. He knew Cecil was right. He *was* hooked, and if he had to take a little poking from the guys, well, that was all right, too. So he rejoined the group and laughed right along with the best of them.

Later, as the evening progressed and other riders bucked out into the arena, Chris walked behind the chutes watching the older, more experienced cowboys. Occasionally, he would stop to ask a question of one of these veterans as he had done in the past. But he noticed when they answered him, they no longer talked down to him: they talked right to him. By demonstrating the courage to climb down on a wild bull, he had proven himself as a cowboy, and was accepted now by the experienced hands he had always admired. He really felt good tonight!

Later that evening, as Chris camped out under the stars behind the arena, he thought back on his younger days, the years he had spent moving all over the country—even to France—following his father's air force career. He was glad when his father had decided to retire, and particularly glad that he chose to retire here in Austin, Texas—truly "cowboy" country.

His favorite memories were of the times the family spent on his Grandpa Gingrich's farm in Michigan and the genuine caring he found there. He could still taste Grandma's fresh-baked biscuits, and he fondly remembered the times that

Grandpa had taken him out on the tractor to work the fields, stopping at the old apple tree to pluck a nice, ripe apple for them to share as they worked.

Watching the stars glitter in the dark, cloudless sky as he lay back in his sleeping bag, Chris's mind was filled with memories of the farm. He smiled to himself as he thought of the time that he, his brother Mike and their Uncle John roped a few calves and rode them in the corral.

It had been a lazy summer afternoon, right after lunch, when Chris and Mike decided to wander over by the barn to watch the young calves. In a few minutes their young Uncle John walked up.

"You know, boys, we ought to grab us a rope and go for a ride on one or two of these calves," John said, sweeping a hand in the direction of the small herd.

The two boys looked at each other, then at their uncle, who was only a few years older than themselves. "What do you mean, Uncle John?" they said, almost in unison.

"Well, you take a piece of cotton rope, loop it around his belly, climb on board and just see how long you can stay on," replied John. "Of course, somebody has to keep a watch out for grown-ups."

Chris and Mike grinned at each other mischievously, then darted off in search of the rope. Within a few minutes they had returned and checked all around for adults. None being found, they turned to John expectantly.

John stepped into the corral and signaled for the boys to follow. The three of them then proceeded to catch a calf and wrestle it to a standstill. John slipped the rope around it and quickly climbed on board the animal to "show the boys how it's done!" He was quickly and unceremoniously dumped in the dirt. Seeing that, Chris was not too eager to try the new "sport" and elected to watch for another time or two, while Mike and John took turns. Finally, to end the taunting and accusations of cowardice, Chris relented and agreed to take a turn.

He soon found himself on top of a squirming bovine with his hand securely strapped into place. Chris nodded his head firmly, and the other two boys fell away from the calf. The contest was on! It lasted only a brief few seconds, but the dislodged rider quickly jumped back to his feet and dusted off his pride. Not one to give up easily, Chris decided to give it another go.

Taking turns, the boys grew better and better, and by the time the sun began to sink into the western sky, all three were fairly covered with bruises, bumps, cuts, dirt and manure. When they finally climbed out of the corral, their toothy grins gave away the fact that they had all had a new world opened up to them: the world of roughstock riding.

The farm had ignited within Chris a feeling he could scarcely understand. But it was a good feeling, and Chris resolved to someday make a home for himself in a place where he could put down roots, raise a family, and make a living with his hands, working the land and raising livestock.

As an orange Texas moon climbed slowly into the night sky, Chris's thoughts drifted along to the time when, shortly after the family moved here to Austin, his grandparents had come from Michigan for a visit.

Their new neighborhood was quite "countrified," with nearly all the families except the LeDouxs having horses or other livestock. With Al LeDoux starting a new job in the real estate business and the rest of the family still settling in, there hadn't been time to investigate the horse market. They all wanted horses, especially young Chris.

Chris was really happy to see his grandparents again, although he wished he could have gone to Michigan instead of having them come down to Texas. His grandfather seemed to sense how much he missed the farm, and he called the young man to his side one afternoon as they sat out on the porch.

"Well, Chris, what do you think of your new home here?" Grandpa asked him.

"Oh, it's okay, I guess, but it'll never compare to the farm," Chris replied.

"You know, Chris, the farm didn't start out the way you see it now," said Grandpa. "When I first moved your grandmother out to that place, it was just a house and a barn and a few acres of land. It didn't really get to be a 'home' for many years, not until we had celebrated a few birthdays, watched new crops come up in the spring, worked the fields during the summer, put away the harvest a few times, seen Christmas come and go, suffered a few setbacks and disappointments, and had many, many good times. All these things had to happen before we could look upon that place as 'home'.

"You see, you only get out of a place what you put into it—just like life," he finished.

Chris had listened to his grandfather with a growing sense of admiration, but countered with "Yeah, but at least you had the land to farm and the livestock to tend. I don't even have a horse or nothin'."

Their conversation was interrupted by a call to supper, but as Grandpa got to his feet, he placed his arm around young Chris and patted him on the shoulder. "I know what you're going through, boy, and I think I know what'll help."

Puzzled, Chris turned to face the man, but no matter how hard he tried, he could not get Grandpa to tell him what he had in mind.

The next morning after breakfast, Al called Chris out onto the porch. "Your grandpa and I thought we'd go over and look at some horses and thought you might like to come along," stated the elder LeDoux.

"Hot dog!" Chris cried, unable to control his enthusiasm.

Soon, the three had piled into the family car and headed out. Just a few miles up the road, Al turned into the driveway of a small ranch. As they pulled to a stop, Chris saw a long barn out behind a red brick house. A man in his mid-thirties was throwing hay from the back of a truck into the depths of one of many outbuildings.

When they got out of the car, the man jumped down and walked over to greet them. The men talked briefly, and the owner of the ranch pointed toward the barn.

"The buckskin would be there . . . third one down." he said. "Saddle goes with the deal, and if you like we can put it on him and let the boy take him out for a ride."

Chris remembered rushing over to the stall to look at the buckskin gelding and thinking how beautiful it was. Soon he was in the saddle, loping out on the driveway and having a ball! By the time he returned to the barn, the owner had gone back to the pickup truck, and Al and Grandpa were smiling at Chris.

"Well, I suppose you'd better get started back toward the house, Chris," Al told him. "It'll take you longer on horseback than it'll take us in the car."

A big smile broke across Chris's face as he kicked the little horse into a run down the lane. "Yippee!" he whooped.

He hadn't found out until much later that his grandfather had paid for the horse, which Chris named Comanche. It was a gift he would never forget.

Comanche changed his life forever. Chris learned to ride and made friends with other young horse owners in the neighborhood. They formed a drill team and learned all sorts of fancy maneuvers together. Eventually, they were invited to entertain at a Boy Scout rodeo, with free entry fees in the events as compensation for their performances.

Chris entered six events, including steer riding, pole bending, barrel racing, ring lancing and goat tying, and he ended up winning four of the six, plus the All-Around Cowboy award. He was presented with four tin belt buckles and a trophy. His first rodeo had really made a mark on him. Of course, the Boy Scouts hadn't been too pleased, because Chris and his friends had won nearly all the prizes, but for Chris it created a new love—rodeo!

Later that summer Chris entered another rodeo a few miles from home, intending to stage a repeat performance of the Boy Scout rodeo. He and his friends arrived at the rodeo grounds hours before the show and wandered behind the chutes. Like all of the other "cowboys," they picked out their personal choices among the "roughstock" calves and steers. Then, since none of them was too experienced, they shared ideas for staying on until the whistle blew.

When it finally came time for the big ride, Chris slipped his rope around the steer he had drawn and had a buddy "pull 'er tight." Then he nodded his head and made a dive into the arena. That was all it took, and the young cowboy was flung into the dirt. At that moment, he realized there was going to have to be some work before he could start riding consistently and winning regularly. Chris spent the rest of the afternoon watching the bigger cowboys rope, ride and tie livestock, trying to absorb as much as he could. He wanted to try it all!

Later, at home, he built a tying dummy: a three-legged critter which could be flipped and tied like a calf. After strapping his saddle to a bale of hay, he practiced by sitting in the saddle and roping his sister's rocking horse, then running over to the tying dummy and flipping and tying it. Practicing in this manner, he became fairly accurate with his old grass rope.

At his next rodeo, this time at the Oak Hill Arena just a few miles from home, he entered several events and won second place in the steer riding. But more importantly, he made friends with some of the local cowboys, who invited him back to Oak Hill for the weekly roping practices. At fifty cents a throw, Chris decided to give it a whirl.

The following Saturday Chris saddled up Comanche, tied a bedroll behind with a can of ravioli tucked inside, and headed off to the arena. Since it took a couple of hours to ride the distance, he had made plans to just camp out at Oak Hill and ride back in the morning. It was a scene he would repeat many, many times during the ensuing months.

Chris had become friends with Cecil Hill, who showed him lots of tricks of the roping trade, like soaking his rope in a water trough and letting it dry to stiffen it up a bit. Chris became a regular at the practice sessions, backing his buckskin into the roping box, then roaring out after an elusive calf. Occasionally, he actually caught the calf, in which case he would need a little help to catch and throw the beast, which usually weighed between two and three hundred pounds. But he never needed help with the half-hitch, not after all those hours on the practice dummy.

Chris usually ran out of money long before he ran out of try, but Cecil would call his number a few more times anyway, just to give the youngster some support. All the hands at Oak Hill were very helpful, especially Cecil, who seemed to sense the potential in Chris.

After each practice session was over, Chris would stake out his horse under the trees, eat cold ravioli from a can, then crawl into his bedroll. At first light he'd be saddled up and on his way home.

Sometimes a stock contractor would bring a load of bulls or bucking horses out to the arena for some practice rough-stock riding. This had been the case earlier tonight; he had been riding steers for some time, but never a real bull.

It just so happened that Al and Chris's mother, Bonnie, had driven out to watch Chris rope that night, and when Chris saw the bulls in the chute, he ran over to his parents and pleaded with them to let him ride a bull.

"Okay, okay Chris. You go ride one of those bulls. Maybe if he gets after you, it'll get this notion out of your mind once and for all!" Al said, handing Chris the three dollars needed to pay for the practice ride. Then he added, "But you be extra careful now, and listen to Cecil."

That had only been a few hours ago, he thought to himself as he lay in his bedroll. The moon was now high in the sky, and quiet had covered the night like a blanket. He still felt a warm glow inside from the way he had been taken into the fold by the veteran cowboys after his brief "crack-out" ride.

Still not quite ready for sleep, Chris pulled out a harmonica his mother had bought for him. Somewhere during all the rodeoing and roping, Chris had also acquired a love for music. Every day he played the harmonica or sang to Comanche. Usually he sang songs that reflected how he felt at any particular time. On the long, solitary rides to and from Oak Hill, he sometimes sang, "Oh, Lonesome Me" or "Cowboy in a Continental Suit."

Soon, the harmonica was returned to his saddle bag, and the young cowboy drifted off to sleep. In the morning he would be saddled and cutting a trail by first light, just as always, but this time it would be just a little different . . . *he* was just a little different. Now, he wasn't just *like* a cowboy, he *was* a cowboy.

The cowboys practiced every Wednesday and Saturday night at Oak Hill, when there wasn't a rodeo in town, and Chris managed to ride up there at least once a week on his buckskin for some roping, riding and camping-out under the stars. It was a magical time for Chris, who learned a great deal about rodeo—and about life—from the old timers and top hands who would always show up. He listened with fascination to their every word, and watched with growing determination as they roped, tied and rode roughstock. Meanwhile, Chris continued to practice at home; although he must have won a thousand rodeos in his mind, he never let up.

About this time, he went down to Buck Steiner's Saddle Shop and bought his first bareback rigging. It was primitive by today's standards, but for young Chris it was "just right." It had a short leather body about eight inches from front to back and perhaps eighteen inches from side to side, somewhat diamond shaped if laid out flat. A pliable leather handle was attached to the body, and two D-rings were stitched onto either side. To each of these rings Chris affixed a long leather latigo, or strap, about two inches wide and four to six feet long. He also bought a cinch to complete the surcingle, which was basically two round rings held together by dozens of soft cotton cords, each the thickness of heavy yarn and about sixteen inches long.

When fully assembled and in place, the cinch is designed to be centered on the chest of the horse, just behind the front legs, with the rings coming halfway up the sides of the horse.

The rigging body sits atop the horse's whithers, centered on his back, and the latigos, hanging from either side, are passed through the rings of the cinch and back up to the rigging, where they are tightened and secured with a Windsor knot. A soft pad sits under the rigging body, and the soft cotton cinch underneath ensures that the outfit does not cause any discomfort to the horse.

Chris spent hours rigging up Comanche and riding him out across the fields of central Texas, all the while imagining a wild ride aboard a top cayuse in someone's bucking string. He soon became very adept at quickly and properly rigging up the horse.

As the summer days waned, Chris continued to sign up for more rodeos, entering the steer riding event. It was to be recorded as a "learning year" for Chris, for he never did make a clean sweep of the awards as he had done at the Boy Scout Rodeo earlier that year.

Cooler weather soon descended on central Texas, and the LeDouxs found that, even as civilians, their nomadic life was far from over; Al had decided that real estate wasn't much of a career for him. He had been offered a position with the American Cancer Society, which would require a move to Denison, Texas, just a few miles from the Oklahoma border, near Lake Texhoma. The family was disconcerted at the prospect of moving once again as they had really begun to put down roots in the Austin area, but economic realities had to be faced. Soon Al, Bonnie and the LeDoux children were on the road once again.

Before the boxes were fully unpacked at the new home, Chris was busy searching for a new arena so that he and Comanche could get back into practice. Soon, his persistence paid off.

"Hey, Mom!" he announced as he burst through the front door. "I found an arena!"

Bonnie dried her hands on her apron and walked out of the kitchen, but before she could speak, the teenager descended on his father, who was sitting quietly in the living room reading the paper.

"Just across the river, in Burns Run, Oklahoma. They got a jackpot every weekend," he explained, as Al peered over the top of his paper.

And the following weekend found Chris hiking over to Burns Run for the weekend jackpot. The arena rotated weekly between a saddlebronc riding contest and a bareback riding contest, with an occasional bull jackpot or regular mixed event rodeo thrown in.

Chris's first day at Burns Run turned out to be on a saddle-bronc weekend. He had never tried the event before, but he had come to ride, so he paid his three dollars: two of which went into the "pot," the last to the contractor who owned the livestock. The contestants shared a single "Turtle" saddle, so named for the original "Turtle Association," predecessor to the Rodeo Cowboys Association, and the first approved competition saddle.

When Chris's turn rolled around, the saddle was thrown atop his horse and cinched up while Chris lowered himself down into the chute. Being younger and somewhat smaller than the rest of the cowboys, some adjustments had to be made to the stirrups while in the chutes, a very dangerous thing to do, but Chris did what he had to. Finally, with several cowboys giving a hand, he was ready for a last-minute briefing from one of the veteran cowboys.

"Well son, the thing to do in this bronc ridin'," said the older man as he handed the bronc reign over to Chris, "is, when he turns out of there, you reach up and get a-holt of him with your spurs and keep in the front end for about three jumps."

"Well, all right," Chris responded uncertainly.

"Now, after those three jumps," the old hand continued, "you just drag 'em out of there and just ... well, just go ahead."

Feeling as sure as any thirteen-year-old novice can feel, Chris nodded his head. The gate cracked open a little bit and the seasoned bronc smashed into it, eager to get out into the arena.

Following instructions, Chris reached up with his spurs and planted them high on the bronc's shoulders for a full three jumps. Then he pulled them out to start spurring front to back, as he knew he should. Suddenly, the horse turned back into a spin. The young rider lost his balance and went tumbling toward the dirt, but one boot was still planted firmly in the stirrup. Chris looked like a rag doll held by the foot, flopping about the arena, just inches from those deadly hooves. The spinning beast was relentless, kicking and stepping on the boy several times and nearly tearing off his shirt. After what seemed an eternity, his foot broke loose and Chris rolled to safety.

Unbelievably, he wasn't seriously injured, but he had had enough of bronc riding for a while and swore off of bucking horses and bulls. Instead of the roughstock, he promised himself to stick with Comanche and just rope, a vow he was to keep for a full two weeks—until the hurt was healed and he found himself again at the arena.

This time when he arrived, he found a full-scale rodeo was about to begin, and after talking it over with his father, Chris sought out the stock contractor to see if he could get entered. He was told the entries were already closed, but if he were to hang around behind the chutes, there just might be a turn-out horse, one the drawn rider had not shown up to claim, and one Chris might be allowed to get on for practice.

Chris picked out a piece of arena fence just down from the bucking chutes and climbed up to watch the rodeo. Each time a bareback rider cracked a gate, Chris mentally placed himself on that horse and lived each ride as if he were the one doing the spurring. No one had ever sat down and explained all the rules to Chris, but from watching the riders, it became apparent to him what had to be done. Suddenly, his thoughts were distracted by a tug on his arm.

"You still wantin' to get on one of these bareback horses, boy?" asked the stock contractor.

"Shoot, yeah!" cried Chris, jumping down from his perch.

"Right down there, in chute five—a white mare. Go get your riggin' on her, and I'll be down in a few minutes to help you get out."

Chris ran over to where he had stashed his rigging and easily picked out the mare. He was so excited at being in an actual rodeo, he "plumb forgot" to be scared; he just put the rigging on the mare, the same way he had pulled it onto Comanche a hundred times before. He looked up to see the rider in the chute ahead of him go out, then lowered himself down onto the horse.

Suddenly, there was a crowd of people around him as the contractor readied the flank strap and the gate men prepared to jerk open the gate to turn the horse into the arena. Chris ran his hand into the rigging handle, to which he had applied a generous amount of tape, sticky side out. (This practice, which was standard in in the early sixties, has since been abolished with the advent of the new "pipe rigging," or hard-handled rigging of the eighties.)

With a quick look into the arena, young Chris nodded his head. The gate cracked open, and he knew he was supposed to reach for the neck with his spurs, so he did—but after that it became a blur. He could feel himself moving to the right, just a little at first ... then he was off! Chris flopped onto the soft arena dirt and scrambled to his feet, unhurt.

Looking down from the bleachers, Al noticed the big grin plastered across Chris's face, and he knew then that there'd be no holding him back after this. All the way home, Chris relived every moment of the ride: his first real rodeo, even if it was just a turn-out ride. It was great!

A few weeks later Chris entered a rodeo in Durant, Oklahoma, as a contestant, and the whole family piled into the car and made the trip. They found the arena to be an old, beat-up facility in what appeared to be someone's backyard.

The bleachers were falling apart and the bucking chutes were in awful shape, but Chris was tickled to death at the prospect of actually getting entered in the rodeo and couldn't care less!

He had drawn a yellow horse for his first head in this two-go-around rodeo and made a pretty good ride. At least he made it to the whistle; even though he hadn't spurred the animal at all during the ride, he was still pleased with himself. Then the pick-up man came around to try to help the boy to the ground. Chris didn't know what to do. He'd never made it this far before. While he sat on the running horse uncertainly, the old-timer plucked him from his perch and dropped him to the ground. It wasn't pretty to watch as the youngster tumbled through the dirt, but he was unhurt, and Chris, not knowing any better, thought he'd done just fine.

Rolling quickly to his feet, the eager LeDoux strained his ears to hear the announcer call out his score.

"... And that last cowboy gets a big goose-egg, ladies and gentlemen. The judges say LeDoux failed to start his horse out of the chute. Let's have a nice round of applause for this young man—that's all he'll take home today...."

Chris was devastated! He was certain he had placed his feet up over the neck and shoulders, and *couldn't* have missed him out. But then there wasn't much use arguing with the judges, so Chris just made up his mind to make up for it on his next ride.

The following day Chris drew a big bay mare in the first section, or group, of barebacks. He pulled his rigging up tight and lowered himself down onto the horse. He looked up in time to see the cowboy ahead of him nod his head and get turned loose into the arena. Metal clanged and horses snorted, and soon a rush of people surrounded Chris in a scene which would soon become routine for the young cowboy:

"Let's go cowboy, get yourself set...."

"Roll that flank strap, hostler . . ."

"Arena's clear—slide and ride, cowboy...."

"Make a good ride, try hard...."

"We're ready, cowboy, let's get outside...."

Everyone seemed to be talking at once, but it was as if they were in another place or time as Chris focused on the job that lay ahead for him. He remembered all his instructions and pulled his hat down snugly over his ears. His left hand was run firmly into the handhold and cracked back to set the "stick." Then, with feet still on the gate rails, he slid up onto the rigging until he was almost sitting on his hand. Carefully, he turned his feet into the chute and clutched the mare's neck with his knees.

"Watch 'em spurs, cowboy. She'll blow up on ye, if'n ye stick 'er."

"Let's go, let's go. Judges are ready."

One quick look into the arena and Chris jerked his head up and down. The latch slammed free with a loud clang as the gate man whipped the gate fully open. The horse hesitated just a second, then the flank strap was pulled up tight and the animal stumbled into the arena, gaining momentum. After two or three long strides, it planted its feet and exploded straight up into the air. The rider was thrown into his rigging, rolling forward slightly, then he regained his balance as his legs slipped back onto the shoulders. The horse turned slightly to the right and fell into an easy "jump-kick" stride, which helped Chris stay centered on the beast. After an eternity the buzzer sounded, and LeDoux reached up with his free right hand and took a double-grip on the rigging handle. As he pulled himself upright and removed the annoying spurs from the horse's neck, the mare stopped bucking and bolted into a run around the arena. The pick-up man maneuvered into place, and Chris again found himself being snatched from the horse's back and tossed to the ground, away from the path of the charging steeds.

Rolling easily to his feet, Chris responded shyly to the spattering of applause from the crowd, looking away from the bleachers as he trotted across the arena to retrieve his misplaced hat.

Suddenly the loudspeaker crackled to life, and Chris's heart froze for a moment as he waited for his score...

"How about a nice round of applause for this young cowboy, ladies and gentlemen. The judges say he missed his mark and will get a no-score. In the bareback riding, a rider is required to 'start his mount,' which means that...."

Chris shook his head in disbelief. Two horses in a row! He was sure he had had his feet out over the neck and shoulders, since he had squeezed his knees together extra hard in the chute as he was nodding his head. Thinking perhaps there was more to this "mark" or "start" than he was aware, he wandered back behind the chutes looking for someone to ask.

Walking casually over to the stripping chute to claim his rigging after it had been taken off the bay horse, Chris scanned the faces for someone who looked familiar enough to be asked a question, yet compassionate enough not to laugh at him for his ignorance. He found the answer to his dilemma when he saw David and Alvin Glover working on a bull rope behind the stock pens. Chris knew David to be one of the top hands in rodeo at that time, so he walked right up and just blurted out, "Say, just how the heck do you go about 'starting' your horse out?"

"Well, son, just go get on a bale of hay and spur it. That's what you need to do, is go practice on a bale of hay," replied David earnestly, looking up from his work just long enough to give Chris a reassuring wink.

"Make sure you get a good grip with your *spurs*, cowboy. Pull yourself up into your rigging with them spurs in his neck—that'll do the trick," added Alvin. "But, like David said, you'd best grab a bale of hay and practice."

"Thanks. I will," Chris replied with a grin. Then he turned away to trot off toward his parents, who, he knew, would be waiting for him in the bleachers.

"Daggone! You gotta have your spurs *in* his neck." Chris thought to himself. "No wonder I didn't mark them horses out. I just had a good leglock on his neck with m' knees. I figured all y' had to do was keep your hooks out *over* his shoulder; I didn't know you actually had to be touching him with your spurs. Shoot, this changes everything!''

As the summer of 1963 wore on, Chris continued to ride his share of the saddlebroncs and bareback horses at Burns Run and sallied forth to nearby towns for an occasional open rodeo or a Little Britches Rodeo Association sanctioned rodeo for contestants less than sixteen years old. When not on roughstock, Chris practiced his bareback riding by rigging up and spurring bales of hay. He was totally ruthless, ripping more than a dozen bales apart with his spurs, then tossing the shredded hay into a stack to be fed to the horses.

The effort finally began to have an effect on the young cowboy. Each time he ''nodded his head'' on a bale of hay he could feel the ''horse'' pulling him into the arena. He could almost sense the rippling neck and shoulder muscles as they worked to free the beast from the lethal grip of Chris's spurs. The cowboy held tight with his feet for two, sometimes three jumps, making certain he had a good ''mark'' before dragging them back toward his rigging and starting his spurring. Then, for ten or fifteen seconds he would rake the ''animal'' by dragging his spurs from the point of the shoulders up the neck to the top of his rigging, only to throw his feet back down again, ''sticking'' the bale of hay in the point of the shoulder again to drag them up the neck to the rigging. Over and over he would repeat the spur-ride as his reflexes began to develop. Soon, spurring became an automatic motion.

''Pull on your riggin', get a lot of drag on your spurs. Throw 'em back down and get ahold again,'' he'd mutter to himself. Even when he wasn't on a bale of hay or rigging up Comanche, riding without spurs, his thoughts were riveted on that rigging, and on the ride. He lived for the opportunity to ''get on another one.''

Late that summer Chris heard about a jackpot rodeo in Colbert, Oklahoma. Jackpot rodeos were different from regular rodeos because there wasn't any prize money added by the rodeo committee or stock contractor, and only the first place winner in each event collected any money. The contestants paid a certain amount of money to ride, and except for a small amount held out to pay the stock contractor for bringing the livestock, the rest went into a "jackpot" for each event, winner-take-all.

Chris hitched a ride with a friend over to Colbert and managed to get entered in the bareback riding. Hoyt Wynette, the stock contractor and acting rodeo secretary, took the cowboys' money and got them all signed up in their events about an hour before the first horses would come pounding up the alleyway into the chutes. When the entries were closed, Hoyt and one of the judges placed numbered poker chips, each representing a different horse, into a hat and randomly drew stock for each contestant. Then they posted the results behind the chutes for the contestants to see.

Chris singled out his draw, a big dun gelding, and he threw his rigging onto the animal's withers. On the far side of the horse the latigo had already been looped through one of the D-rings in his cinch; together they hung nearly to the ground. Taking a long wire hook, Chris reached under the horse and snared the cinch, bringing it under the animal. Next he took the loose latigo from the near side of the bronc and ran it through the other D-ring in the cinch, then back up to the rigging—a pass through the ring of the rigging, then another loop through the cinch and back up to the top again. The end of the latigo was tucked into the rigging and the rigging was allowed to sit loose while Chris and the other bareback riders got spurred-up and made last minute adjustments to their equipment.

Finally, the call from the arena director: "Pull 'em up, boys. We're ready to rodeo!"

Chris was second in line to go, so he quickly tightened up the rigging, making sure that it was up high enough on the withers and dead center, and checked to make sure the cinch was centered underneath the horse. Assured that everything was just right, he pulled on his glove and wrapped the leather thong around his wrist to keep the glove from slipping.

Making a quick mental check of equipment from head to toe, he climbed over the dun and slowly lowered himself down into the chute. He put most of his weight on the horse, sitting back from his rigging with his feet resting on the gate rails and being very careful not to let his spurs accidentally touch the animal. Chris used his knees to gently rock the horse from side to side to relax the animal as he looked up at the rider ahead of him in the first chute. He could see the rider was having a problem with his rigging and was nowhere near ready, so Chris slid back just a bit to wait.

"Let's go on to number two, that cowboy's about set to go," someone called from the arena. Suddenly the chute help abandoned the first chute and moved into position on Chris's.

Chris reached up, ran his hand into the handle of his rigging and slid up onto the withers, nearly sitting on his riding hand. Rehearsing the "start" in his mind, he closed his eyes for just an instant. When he opened them he picked out a spot on the horse's neck to watch, then nodded his head.

Chris's legs shot up, and with toes out he grabbed the horse in the point of the shoulder, a natural pocket, and held tight for two full jumps. The horse then broke into a smooth bucking action. Chris took advantage of all his practice, dragging his spurs up as the animal reared into a high dive, slamming his spurs back into its neck as its front feet hit during a high kick.

"Stick 'em. Drag 'em. Throw 'em back down and get ahold again," he said to himself. He could see sky and occasionally the tops of the empty bleachers as he lay back kicking and spurring. Then, in the space of a single held breath, the whistle sounded and it was all over ... well, almost over. For all his practice at *riding*, Chris still hadn't figured out how to contend with pick-up men, who moved in to retrieve a cowboy when a successful ride was over.

The pick-up man rode up next to Chris's dun and half grabbed and half knocked the young cowboy into the dirt. Staggering back to his feet indignantly, Chris's bruised feelings were soon appeased by the announcement of his score.

"Put the kid down for a sixty-five," he heard one of the judges say to the rodeo secretary.

Now began the waiting game. He was the first rider, the first with a score, so he was in first place! If everyone else bucked off, fouled, or scored worse than him, he could win the whole jackpot. He knew that out of a possible hundred points, his score was very average, and not usually good enough to win, but there were only three other contestants, so he figured it might just hold up. He grabbed a good seat and watched the rest of the bareback riding. Two of the riders bucked off, and the third almost did, which resulted in a very low score. Chris LeDoux was the winner of the bareback riding jackpot!

He raced over to the rodeo secretary and collected his eight dollars as enthusiastically as if it had been eight thousand. His first prize money! He ran home and tucked one of the dollar bills into a scrapbook, where it would remain for the rest of his life.

If he had been in love with the sport before, he now became passionately devoted to riding roughstock. Every weekend found him at a jackpot in Colbert or Burns Run, and, while he won a few and lost a few, he began developing a sound system for riding the barebacks.

He also experimented with different ways of dismounting after the ride. Having had a few "wrecks" with pick-up men, Chris tried a bevy of alternatives. This experimentation resulted in his tearing open his hand on a fence on one occasion, and getting the wind knocked out of him numerous times from "flying dismounts" of his own design. He soon decided that maybe the pick-up men weren't so bad after all. Then he began to watch some of the better cowboys and the finesse with which they dismounted. Not surprisingly, he finally caught on.

Chris's first solo outing came when he heard of a Little Britches sanctioned rodeo in Anadarko, Oklahoma, which was several hundred miles away. Swayed by the boy's impassioned pleas, Al finally consented to letting Chris enter but couldn't take the time off to drive him up to Anadarko, so they bought Chris a bus ticket and sent him on his way.

The young cowboy stowed his rigging, a change of clothes, a pup-tent, and a can of pork-n-beans, in case he got hungry, in his mother's laundry bag. He took a short hop over to Sherman, Texas, then had to change bus lines for the ride to Anadarko. This also meant changing bus depots, so on arrival at Sherman, Chris stuffed his ticket in his back pocket, tossed his laundry bag over his shoulder, and headed across town on foot.

He arrived at the new bus station with just a few minutes to spare; his bus was already loading for departure. He rushed to the ticket counter—and discovered his ticket was missing! Chris dug in every pocket, nook and cranny, all to no avail. He must have dropped it somewhere between stations, so he turned around and back-tracked his route.

Chris lucked out and found the ticket in an empty lot, but by the time he got back to the depot his bus had already left. Desperate to get to the rodeo, he asked the ticket agent when the next bus would be leaving for Anadarko. The time of departure was many hours away, and the bus would not arrive in Anadarko until exactly 8:00 p.m., which was precisely the time the rodeo was to start. Chris exchanged his ticket and hoped he could still make it in time to ride.

With a lot of time to kill, he took out the rodeo poster and found a phone number to the rodeo secretary, who told him they would wait as long as they could. She also promised to send someone down to the bus depot in Anadarko to pick him up and bring him to the rodeo.

A few hours later Chris was aboard the bus. When he arrived in Anadarko, he was met by the parents of one of the local contestants. Tossing Chris's gear into the back of the

car, they made a dash for the rodeo grounds. Gravel spray-
ing every which way, the car pulled into the contestant area,
and Chris's horse—alone—was standing in a chute. Hurried-
ly he threw his rigging on the animal, even though all the other
bareback riders had already had their turns and the ropers
were now out in the arena. When the rigging was set, Chris
put on his spurs and glove, and climbed up onto the chute
to let the arena boss know everything was ready.

After the ropers cleared the arena, the chute crew came over
to Chris and made final preparations for the ride. Chris didn't
have the vaguest idea of how his competition stacked up, so
he knew he had to put everything he could into the ride.

He nodded his head and stuck the spurs into the pocket,
just the way he should. The bronc turned back hard, just outside the gate, and threw Chris into the dirt.

"What a day," Chris thought as he brushed off the dirt
and manure and headed back behind the chutes. After watching the rest of the show, he picked out a suitable location for
his campsite and pitched his tent. One of the locals saw him
and invited him home for dinner—an offer Chris readily
accepted.

Dinner was excellent, and Chris was beginning to discover
another side of rodeo he had never seen before: the camaraderie and kinship a cowboy "on the road" finds whenever
he pulls into the rodeo grounds. It seems the locals have all
been down that lonesome road before, so when the rodeo is
in their hometown, they extend all the hospitality they can
to the other cowboys. Relatives may be hundreds of miles
away, but "family" can always be found at any rodeo!

The next day, Chris was less rushed and had a chance to
get into the proper frame of mind before his second go-around.
He slipped down onto the yellow stud and gave him his very
best ride. Although he didn't win anything, riding in the rodeo
had qualified Chris for the National Little Britches Finals in
Littleton, Colorado, later that fall.

On the bus ride home that night, Chris had a chance to look
back over the entire weekend and sort out all of the details,

reliving and savoring each moment. The riding could have been better, but the friends he'd found and the feeling of being with family were exhilarating. It was an unexpected and wonderful discovery. He knew that no matter where he was, and no matter how far from Bonnie and Al he wandered, home, for him, would be just a rodeo away.

Chapter 2

So You Want To Be a Cowboy

So you want to be a cowboy, and you want to rodeo?
Well, I don't see nothing to hold you back, just pack your
bags and go.
You'll travel many highways, and boy, you're gonna see it all,
You'll have yourself some good times, but you're gonna take
some falls.

Now, lay off hard liquor, and leave them pills alone,
They'll only dull the senses and leave you weak and stoned.
If you want to be a winner, son, you've got to play it straight,
Give it everything you've got when they open up the gate.

Well, there ain't no easy goin' on the rodeo trail,
And for every man that's made it, a hundred men have failed.
But, if you're mighty lucky, and you've got a lot of try,
There's a big gold buckle waiting at the end of the line.

Chris LeDoux (Wyoming Brand Music)
from **He Rides the Wild Horses**

The Little Britches National Finals was a long way to travel, and it was no easy task for a young cowboy to talk his folks into making a trip of that distance just for a rodeo. But luck was with Chris that year.

The LeDouxs had been planning a vacation that would combine a bit of business with pleasure, as Al needed to go to Casper, Wyoming, for a job interview. With Chris's persistence, a leg was added to the trip which would put them in Littleton, Colorado, at the appropriate time.

While it may have been an enjoyable family outing, Chris's mind kept wandering off to the rodeo grounds, picturing what it would be like and how he would ride. He must have lived through that ride a hundred times, and every time he came up a winner!

Having never really been exposed to a lot of kids his own age who competed in rodeo, Chris often wondered just how he would fit in. He wondered what his own style and skill would look like compared to the boys he would meet at the finals who had learned their skills in various parts of the country. But he knew that no matter how he looked, talked or acted, everything really depended on how he could ride. He was determined to be the very best rider he could be, and if that wasn't good enough . . . well, he would always know he had given it everything he had.

When he arrived at Littleton, Chris was relieved to find most of the contestants were cowboys just like him. In fact, he had never seen so many young cowboys in one place before who were so much alike in the ways they dressed, talked and acted—and, most importantly, in how they felt about rodeo.

The LeDouxs set up camp with several other families behind the holding pens. Chris quickly made a few friends and headed over to take a look at the roughstock. As the boys looked over the horses and bulls on which they would be riding, talk soon turned to the competition.

"Well, Chris," one of them began, "you bein' a bareback rider, you need to watch out for Virgil Lawson. Yessir, he's about the best I've ever seen."

"That's right, pard," chimed in another, a self-proclaimed bull rider. "Why, that old boy flat puts the steel to 'em."

Chris nodded his head and listened intently to all they had to say. Being from the same part of the country as the stock contractor, the other boys knew a little bit about some of the stock, and what they didn't know, they just made up as they went along. Soon Chris had a pretty good "feel" for the horses in the herd, and he had his mind made up as to which horse he hoped to draw into.

The Finals Rodeo that year was a one-head show, with each contestant up once and only once in the two-day rodeo. Chris had drawn up for Saturday's show, but if his score was good enough to make the top four, the Sunday competitors would be trying to beat his score and bump him out. As it happened, Virgil Lawson also drew up on Saturday.

Chris had picked out his draw, a bay horse in chute six, and was carefully going over his equipment when over the fence climbed a confident young cowboy, with flashy boots and chaps and an air of superiority about him. He tossed his rigging bag casually to the ground, walked over to take a look at his paint horse, then proceeded to stretch and rosin his bull rope, brush out his chaps, and finally rosin up his bareback rigging. There was no doubt in Chris's mind: this must be Virgil Lawson.

Virgil's horse was in chute five. Chris was glad the young puncher would be going ahead of him so he could see how he rode. Maybe he would buck off and Chris's worries would be over.

Static crackled over the loudspeaker, and after a few garbled words from the announcer, the unmistakable sounds of "The Star Spangled Banner" came floating back behind the chutes. The flurry of activity ceased, as if on cue, and hats were swept from heads to be placed over hearts. Even the horses seemed to sense the solemnity of the moment and stood quietly.

As the last notes of the song faded, the crowd roared its approval, and the "grand entry" of mounted cowboys and cowgirls, who had been standing quietly inside the arena during the Anthem, broke tumultously for the out gate. The arena director came riding by slowly, pausing at each chute.

"Pull 'em tight, boys," he bellowed. "Let's get ready to ride ...."

It was the cue they had all been waiting for for weeks; now, after all that waiting, it seemed as if they didn't have enough time! They scrambled for their chutes, where they had loosely set their riggings in place, and began tightening down on the cinches.

As he was tucking away the last latigo, Chris was startled by the clanging of a chute gate. The first rider was in the arena! Chris knew the first couple of chutes had been given an early signal to "pull 'em up," but he still felt he was behind, and so he hurried himself up. With the rigging set, he pulled himself back out of the chute and walked over to his rigging bag for his glove. The second rider made his bid for the national title. . . .

Chris looked again at Virgil, who was making a final adjustment to his rigging.

"Okay, Chris," he said to himself. "Just relax. You don't go 'til after Lawson, and he's not ready yet. Settle down. Remember the basics: Get a hold with your spurs, drag 'em up, drive 'em back down and get a hold again."

He tucked his glove into his chaps and practiced the spurring action, one leg at a time, running his spur up his boot nearly to his knee, pulling it out and jamming it back into the "horse's neck," then switching feet and going with the other leg.

Chutes three and four had already discharged their riders, and Chris could see that Virgil, in chute five, was nearly ready to go. The rider ahead of him had bucked off quickly, but the horse was still in the arena and the pick-up men were skillfully working the animal towards the stripping chute.

Chris climbed up and over his mount. Reaching down with his right hand he grabbed a handful of mane and began rocking the horse gently back and forth as he lowered himself down. The bay horse snorted and stamped its feet a little but soon calmed back down again as Chris talked to it.

"Easy," he said gently. "If you was scared, you never should have entered this rodeo."

Chris talked absently as his attention was focused on the rider ahead of him; he knew Virgil's ride would be the mark he would have to beat. Suddenly, the rider nodded his head and was turned loose into the arena.

Chris had hoped all of the confidence and swagger he had seen behind the chutes was all just an act, and that the cowboy really wasn't *that* good at the actual riding. There were a lot of showy cowboys: those who had been on one or two head but talked as though they had busted whole herds single handedly. From the very first jump, however, Chris knew everything they had said about Virgil was true. The paint turned hard to the right, and the rider leaned inside with him just a bit as his legs flailed the horse's neck. The toes were pointed ninety degrees off the neck, and the free hand was working thin air, where it was supposed to be, so there was no chance of a foul. The whistle sounded and the crowd jumped to its feet. They had been having problems with the P.A. system all night, and now Chris listened for the score but couldn't make it out. It was good, though, since the crowd reacted again to whatever the announcer had said.

Chris saw the cowboy being swept to the ground by the skilled pick-up man, then he turned his attention back into his own chute. It was all up to him now.

Working at an almost frantic pace, Chris ran his hand deep into his rigging and pulled out the slack in the fingers of his glove. He had pasted a thick coating of sticky pine resin, legal in those days, all over the rigging handle, and now he worked the fingers and palm to a sticky grip. The rider slid forward onto the rigging, reached up with his right hand to pull his hat down tight, took a deep breath, then nodded his head.

The gate cracked open and the bronc turned out hard into the arena. Chris dug his spurs into the animal's neck for a solid "mark" and held them there for a full two jumps; then he began a fluid rake up and down the neck, coming nearly to the withers at the top, then dropping his heels back down again. In just a few seconds the whistle blew, and the ride was over.

Chris pulled himself upright with his free hand and began working at loosening the sticky gloved hand from the handle.

Too late, he saw the well-intentioned pick-up man riding hard toward him. Much like jousting knights in the days of King Arthur, the two cowboys approached each other at a break-neck pace.

"Shoot, there's no way," Chris thought to himself. "I'll get hung up or killed if he reaches for me."

An arm shot out and caught the young bareback rider firmly about the middle. Chris was jerked out of the rigging like a calf hitting the end of a rope, with feet flying everywhere. He was dumped unceremoniously onto the arena dirt, where he did a quick check of his major body parts, fearing an arm or leg had been jerked off completely. There turned out to be nothing more serious than an injury to his pride, however, and Chris picked up his hat and walked quickly back towards the chutes.

The crowd was applauding wildly, but there was no doubt in Chris's mind that his ride couldn't possibly have been as good as Virgil's. He was proud, though; he had done his very best, he was sure of that, and it felt good inside.

Since the family was eager to be getting back home and Chris was sure he hadn't won, the LeDouxs left early the next morning and didn't stay around for Sunday's competition. In fact, they hadn't even paid any attention to the scores which *had* been turned in. If they had, they would have seen Chris's name at the top of the list for Saturday's performance. Chris had beaten out Virgil Lawson, and all of the others. As the family drove down the road towards Texas, Sunday's competitors had all set their sights on beating Chris's score from the day before. None succeeded. Chris LeDoux was the 1964 World Champion Little Britches Bareback Rider—and he didn't even know it!

A week later, Chris received a letter telling him the good news, but even then he refused to believe it—until the buckle arrived. Yes, he really was the world's champ, the cowboy who had won the "big rodeo," and he was absolutely thrilled by it all.

Chris's first memories of Cheyenne, Wyoming, were of the bitter cold in the winter of 1965. He had heard stories about how Wyoming was real "cowboy country" and was a little excited about the prospect of seeing so many cowboys in one place. So he was somewhat disappointed to find that, like Texas, the only real cowboys to be found were out in the hills and valleys, not in the cities. In many respects, Cheyenne was pretty much like the towns in Texas—except for the cold.

"Doggone, it's never been this cold in Texas," said Chris from the back seat of the family car.

"Man on the radio says it's ten below zero," Bonnie replied.

Al just set his lip and didn't say anything. Ever since he had been offered the job in Wyoming, the family took every chance to make it known they weren't pleased about having to move away from Texas.

Al had received a promotion and found a place in a suburb of Cheyenne that would accomodate the family and the horses, but after the years in Texas it took all of them a little while to get used to the ever-present snow and slush. The LeDouxs finally managed to get back into a regular routine, however, and even enjoyed the climate when they would take a trip up to Jackson Hole for some skiing.

The LeDoux children were all enrolled in school and quickly made friends for themselves, but Chris was looking forward to the spring rodeo season getting underway. He passed many an hour kicking a bale of hay or rigging up the buckskin to practice his balance.

Finally, Chris heard about a Little Britches rodeo down in Boulder, Colorado, and talked Al and Bonnie into taking him. All winter Chris had been practicing for the bareback event, but he had also decided to branch out this year into other events. After all, he reasoned, he had so much fun working one event, the more he entered, the more fun it would be . . . or at least that was the logic which he applied.

Chris entered the bull riding, calf roping, saddlebronc riding and, of course, the bareback riding events. As he entered more and more rodeos, he learned that entering multiple events did indeed increase the thrill and excitement of rodeo, but it also meant multiplying the work and pain that goes into each event.

Although he didn't talk about it very much at the time, the truth was, in all his years of riding roughstock, Chris sometimes had a sinking feeling inside when he was about to get on a bronc or a bull.

"What am I doin' here?" he asked himself later as he stood behind the chutes at a rodeo in Laramie, Wyoming. He could feel that gnawing, churning feeling again. Compared to last year and the year before, the anxiety attacks were getting less frequent and less severe, but they still persisted.

In his first year, he felt scared right after entering a rodeo. Now, he didn't really start getting weak-kneed until a few minutes before it was time to get down on his mount. Chris knew he was getting better, and the confidence chipped away at the fear. Someday it would just be a little case of the jitters; all he had to do was to keep "gettin' on 'em" to build in himself that winning character he admired so much in his cowboy heroes.

"When the cravin' to get 'em overcomes the fear ... well, I guess then you're a cowboy," he thought as he lowered himself down into the chute.

Chris spent the rest of the summer going to lots of rodeos and spending countless hours kicking bales of hay. In addition, he built a roping and tying dummy and honed his skills in the calf roping. His diligence paid off handsomely, with prizes won in at least one of his four events at every competition.

Living in Cheyenne, Wyoming, becomes a special treat for rodeo lovers every year when Frontier Park comes alive with the magic of the Cheyenne Frontier Days Rodeo. Chris and the Schaffer brothers, Wess and Mike, set out a few days before the big show for the rodeo grounds. They packed some food in a bedroll and staked out a claim in an unoccupied horse stall, which they called "home" for the better part of the next week.

The only problem the boys had was trying to figure out a way to get into the rodeo itself each day. They had asked for jobs with the contractor, Harry Knight, but all the jobs had been filled. The only other thing they could think of was to enter the wild horse race, but try as they might, they could not figure out a way to come up with the entry fees.

A truckdriver was stretched out nearby listening to the whole convesation, and he was tickled by what he had heard. He could remember a time in his own boyhood when he'd have done anything to get into a rodeo—except buy a ticket!

"Hey boys!" the driver called out. "C'mere a minute."

He offered to pay their fees in the wild horse race. Chris never figured out if he just wanted to help, or whether he wanted to watch a couple of youngsters get killed, but the boys eagerly accepted the offer.

The wild horse race at Cheyenne is an annual ritual, part of the heritage of the Cheyenne Frontier Days celebration. First, wild horses are loaded into the bucking chutes. There they are haltered, with long lead ropes attached. Then the pick-up men dally the lead ropes around their saddlehorns and the horses are individually lead from the chutes to the racetrack adjacent to the rodeo arena.

About fifty yards of track rail are removed to make it easier to get the wild horses onto the track, where they are turned over to their respective three-man teams. As soon as all of the horses have been moved to the track, the rails are replaced, and a gun sounds to start the race. Each team must then attempt to saddle the horse, and one team member must ride the beast completely around the racetrack, one time, and across the finish line.

In 1965, however, the wild horse race didn't come off exactly as it was supposed to, for Chris and his friends weren't quite sure of all of the rules. They had the basics down, but the official "start" of the race is where they blew it.

When the wild horses were brought out, Chris and his friends somehow managed to get their lead rope from the pick-up man while they were still in the rodeo arena. With a wild horse at the end of their rope, the boys figured it was time to start, so they began saddling the horse right away. The horse was very cooperative and stood quietly while the saddle was cinched tight. Then, Chris vaulted into the seat.

The horse took exception to the weight of its rider and began to buck, but Chris was sitting tight. After a few seconds, the horse took off at a dead run down the arena fence and past the bucking chutes. Chris grinned at the cowboys he saw there, who were all howling with laughter at his antics. In a few seconds, he was darting through the gate, out of the rodeo arena and onto the racetrack.

"Look out!" Chris yelled as his horse nearly ran into a few of the people on the track. They scurried for cover, and he was quickly past them.

He headed around the first curve and then down the far straightway.

"The Lone Ranger is way out in front as he presses on the back stretch . . . ," rodeo announcer Chuck Parkinson mocked a racetrack caller. The crowd was really enjoying the action as Chris rounded the last turn and headed for the final quarter of the race.

"Hot dang!" Chris thought to himself. "I'm way out in front." He was elated at being so far ahead of the competition. His glory was short-lived, however, as the gun went off, marking the official start of the race. Chris realized then just how much he had really messed up. He decided to play out the hand and barreled across the finish line with all the gusto of a championship ride. Vaulting to the ground, out of breath and embarrassed, Chris sneaked off behind the chutes as quickly as he could.

His pride was soon mended, however, and the boys were free to wander behind the chutes with the "pros"—those real-live cowboy heroes Chris and his friends had read about in the *Rodeo Sports News* and *Western Horseman Magazine*.

There were dozens of champions, past champions and future champions present at Cheyenne that year, as always: Jim Houston, Johnny Hawkins, Ronnie Rosen, Enoch Walker, Bill Kornell, Guy Weeks—the list was endless. These were the first real champions Chris had ever been close to, and it really made a mark on the young cowboy.

"Out of chute number seven," boomed the voice of Chuck Parkinson over the P.A. system, "a bronc called Come Apart. This horse has been twice-named the RCA Bareback Bucking Horse of the Year, and he's being ridden by a great all-around cowboy: Bill Kornell."

Chris pressed his face close to the fence so he could get a better view of the arena. He couldn't see the chutes very well, but as the gate swung open, Come Apart exploded into the arena. Kornell's spurs were digging into the horse's neck, and Chris could "feel" the entire ride as if *he* were atop the legendary horse. The ride almost seemed to switch into slow motion as the horse jumped and kicked across the arena, trying to unseat the cowboy, but to no avail. The whistle blew, and the pick-up men rushed to his side. In a few seconds, Bill Kornell was on the ground. Chris could see he had hurt his riding arm and was cradling it near his belly. He also noticed that big, shining gold buckle. Even through the pain, Bill managed a weak smile, proud he'd ridden such a legend. Chris also knew that feeling, although on a lesser scale, and he vowed right then that someday he too would wear that gold buckle.

A few weeks after the Frontier Days Rodeo was ended, Chris saddled up Comanche and rode back to Frontier Park. When they arrived, he found the grounds deserted except for a colony of prairie dogs. Some of these would pop up suddenly from their holes, chatter excitedly, then vanish back into the earth again. Chris unsaddled the horse and carefully stowed the gear. He then placed his bareback rigging on the animal and led it into one of the bucking chutes.

Chris started his routine of warm-up exercises and preparations for his "big ride." In his mind he could hear the an nouncer bantering with the sell-out crowd as the clowns hammed it up in the arena.

"Ladies and gentlemen, before you stands proof positive that man indeed is decended from apes...."

Chris slipped his glove on and began to rosin the rigging.

"And now, we have a very special treat for you all, as we move down to the bucking chutes...."

Chris lowered himself down onto Comanche and ran his hand into the rigging, setting his hand firmly.

"Five time World Champion Bareback Rider Chris LeDoux has drawn the top of Harry Knight's bucking string: a horse called Come Apart, twice named Bucking Horse of the Year."

Chris slid up onto the rigging and pulled his hat down tight with his free hand.

"This, ladies and gentlemen, is sure to be recorded as one of the most spectacular match-ups in the history of rodeo."

Chris nodded his head and with his free hand reached down and threw open the gate. Comanche trotted casually out into the arena, with Chris screwed down for a world-class ride.

"Ladies and gentlemen, will you look at that animal buck! Why, if he gets any higher into the air Chris will have to get a pilot's license! It must be like riding an explosion!"

Without spurs, Chris was raking Comanche up the neck. The little buckskin trotted briskly around the arena, looking into the empty bleachers.

"And there's the whistle, folks! Can you believe that incredible performance by both man and beast?"

Chris pulled himself up with his free hand and waved at the crowd of prairie dogs that had gathered to watch this spectacle. Then, imaging himself to be in the company of a skilled pick-up man, he vaulted to the ground.

"He can hear you now, ladies and gentlemen. Let's give him a big round of applause while we wait for the judges' score."

Chris swept his hat from his head and waved it at the imaginary crowd.

"I don't believe this, folks: the judges have awarded LeDoux ninety-four points for that spectacular ride on Come Apart! Chris LeDoux is the winner of the bareback riding event this year!"

He threw his hat high into the air, spinning it like a Frisbee.

"All winners please report to the stage in front of the grandstands to receive your awards."

Chris picked up his hat and moved over to the vacant stage, where a few weeks ago streamers and bunting had hung, and ascended the steps to the small platform. He reached out to shake an imaginary hand and receive an imaginary trophy buckle.

He looked out at the empty bleachers and the vacant bucking chutes and saw throngs of spectators and contestants— all cheering for him! For the first time, he really yearned for one of those gold buckles he had seen a few weeks ago, one that said "World Champion."

With hat in hand and the wind tousling his hair, Chris stood solemnly on the award platform. Even the prairie dogs seemed to sense the seriousness of the occasion and stood quietly at attention. Although he hadn't really won anything that day, he had taken the first step toward becoming a winner for real; on that cool, wind-swept day in Cheyenne, a desire was formed within Chris that would shape the rest of his life, the desire to be World Champion. This dream would provide the fuel to keep the fire lit within the cowboy until the day the gold buckle was really his to keep. Through years of adversity and hardships, of injuries and set-backs, this "Gold Buckle Dream" would stay with him, keeping alive the desire and the determination to win the World.

Chapter 3

A Cowboy's Got To Ride

Well, your mama finds it hard to understand,
Why her lovin' son wants to be a rodeo man.
And your daddy had a whole lot of great big plans for you,
You hate to disappoint him but you got other things to do.

Now your best girl thinks it's time you settled down.
You finally graduated, and she's ready for a wedding gown.
But there's a great big world just waitin' out there for you,
And if she really loved ya, she could wait another year or two.

Now your high school buddies say, "Man, you've gone insane,
Don't you know rodeo's a crazy, foolish game?"
But you can see in their eyes a little bit of jealousy.
They're all working nine to five—you're footloose and
    fancy-free.

Nobody really knows how you feel inside.
The road gets rough, and the going gets tough,
But you know you've got to try.
And there ain't no way they're ever gonna change your mind.
Don't everybody know? A cowboy's got to ride.

Chris LeDoux (Wyoming Brand Music),
from **Thirty Dollar Cowboy**

The spring of 1967 found Al LeDoux in Nashville, having accepted a transfer, while Bonnie and the rest of the family were still in Cheyenne finishing out the school year. Chris, a senior at Cheyenne Central High School, was still riding pretty steadily at high school rodeos while he anxiously waited for school to be over for good.

Going down the rodeo trail regularly, you begin to see the same faces over and over; eventually a cowboy comes to know everyone in his event, and in many other events as well. There's always a new face, but, particularly in a small circuit, the contestants get to know each other pretty well. It was at one of those first high school rodeos, in Casper, that Chris met John "Witch" Holman and John Forbes. They quickly became friends and were soon talking about buying their RCA permits, which would enable them to enter some of the professional rodeos. They also talked of the upcoming Wyoming State High School Finals Rodeo in Cheyenne, which would be held in early June, soon after school got out.

The weeks flew by, and soon Chris found himself at the rodeo grounds for the long-awaited Finals. A few other cowboys had arrived, some with their families, but there weren't any spectators yet. The stock pens were full, but, after a quiet night, the bulls and broncs were standing easy. Chris made his way around behind the bucking chutes to drop off his rigging bag.

Memories began to drift back to him of his many visits to this arena a few years earlier, when his only audience had been a handful of prairie dogs and his old buckskin horse, Comanche. Chris walked casually over to the arena gate. Propping a booted foot on the bottom rail, he rested his chin on crossed arms on another rail. Thus positioned, he peered out across the deserted arena looking at the empty bleachers and the vacant press box. A faint smile played across his lips as he remembered walking up the steps of that press box to receive his imaginary trophy buckle. He looked out the back fence to see a troop of prairie dogs playing blissfully in the early morning sunshine.

Chris chuckled, "I wonder if any of you little fellers remember me?" He though he heard one of them laugh in his direction. "That's right, little pardner, I'm the same kid who used come up here and dream of winning the big trophy buckle. I suppose you've got a right to laugh—I'll bet I was quite a sight, prancing around the arena on old Comanche, but we'll see who's laughing after today. I'm gonna win that buckle for real this time, and you'll be telling all your friends that you used to know me 'way back when'." It wasn't a gold buckle, but the Wyoming State High School Champion buckle wouldn't be bad, he thought.

Chris heard footsteps approaching, and he turned to see Witch Holman and John Forbes coming around the fence. They called out friendly greetings to each other, and after their gear had been stowed they all walked back toward the stock pens to look over the roughstock. Chris glanced back over his shoulder for one last look at the empty arena and those playful prairie dogs out behind the fence, knowing a promise had been made.

The next few hours seemed to drag by. The draw was finally done about an hour before showtime, and the bleachers were beginning to fill up. The announcer had moved into the press box and was busily reviewing the sheaves of paper he had stowed in his brief case. The public address system was turned on and tuned to a popular Country/Western radio station. Chris and the other contestants stretched out their legs and sat on the ground behind the chutes, leaning up against the fences. Some were preparing equipment, but most had already done this at least once already and were now content to just sit idly by and tell rodeo stories to each other. It helped to pass the time and relieved some of the stress which was beginning to build in them all.

Chris half listened to the chatter and half listened to the songs on the radio. Wynn Stewart sang "It's Such a Pretty World, Today," Charlie Pride crooned out "Just Between You and Me," Buck Owens contributed "I've Got a Tiger by the Tail," and several other popular songs filled the air.

Then there was a break in the music as the announcer asked the mounted contestants, who had been warming up their horses, to exit the arena so it could be dragged and watered the final time before the show. (Roughstock riders are not directly affected by this announcement, but as you spend more and more time behind the chutes you begin to listen for certain "signals" from the announcer that let you know just how much time you have before your event. This particular call is a standard that signifies about a half an hour before grand entry.)

With that announcement, the mood behind the chutes visibly shifted as the contestants began going over their equipment one last time and stretching out and warming up in earnest. Chris, too, began warming up and loosening muscles in his legs, back and arms which would soon be taxed to their limits. He applied generous amounts of tape to his wrist to lessen the severe jolt that racks every bareback rider's arm when the horse makes his "high dive" into the arena. A rider's arm can receive close to eight hundred pounds of force with this initial turn into the arena.

"Would all mounted contestants please report to the main arena gate, the grand entry begins in five minutes...," the P.A. system crackled.

Without looking, the roughstock riders knew the grand entry was forming up just outside the gate, and the bareback horses would be coming up the alleyway any second now. Chris slipped his boot and shank straps into place and tightened them down. He reached into his bag and pulled out his chaps, fastening them about his waist, though not yet tightening the leg straps.

The thundering hooves, snorting horses and clanging metal gates signaled it was time for contestants to find their mounts and start rigging up. Chris's draw was in the third chute, pacing nervously in the small enclosure, nostrils flaring. The dust raised by the charging horses had thickened the air behind the chutes until the arena had become a totally different place than

the arena in which the cowboys had relaxed just an hour
before.

Chris picked his rigging off the fence and headed for his
horse. He quickly slid the rigging down onto the nervous
animal, and another cowboy reached with the wire hook to
pull the cinch underneath the animal. Chris instinctively and
adroitly spun the latigo through the D-ring two times, laying
the free end across the hand hold. The rigging thus loosely
fastened, he pulled himself back out of the chute. He knew
the chute boss would tell them when to begin tightening up
the cinches, so he grabbed his rosin bag and went to work
on his glove and hand-hold on the rigging.

He glanced up and down the "line" and saw a flurry of
activity in every direction. Out in the arena, the introductions
were still going on, and mounted dignitaries and pretty young
women were riding around as they were announced, waving
to the crowd.

Suddenly, the first few bars of "The Star Spangled Banner" played across the P.A. system, and the activity stopped
abruptly. The crowd rose to its feet, and hats were swept from
heads to be placed tenderly over loyal, patriotic hearts. Behind
the chutes the scene was pretty much the same: cowboys always
paying respect to the flag many of their fathers and forefathers
had fought and died to preserve.

As he watched the flag bearer parade slowly around the
arena, Chris could feel the hair rise slowly on the back of his
neck, and a tingle coursed through his body. Hearing the National Anthem at a rodeo never failed to bring out that tingl-
ing, for it was one of the times he was especially proud of
being a cowboy, of being able to take part in this celebration
of Americanism. Even though most cowboys didn't talk about
it much, Chris knew all of his friends felt the same.

As the last notes began to fade, the chute boss, who had
been standing in front of chute one, turned to the cowboy in
that hole and signaled for him to pull his rigging up tight. Then
he walked to chute two and made the same motion to that
rider. Chris, who was in the fourth slot, watched all of this,

knowing it would do no good to try to anticipate the chute boss, who wouldn't feel right unless he gave the signal himself. Chris just waited until the man got down to his chute.

"Okay cowboy, pull it up," the chute boss said, getting louder now that the Anthem was ended.

Chris nodded his head and slid down onto the horse's back. The bay mare snorted and pranced nervously in the chute, but Chris talked softly to her, patting her neck reassuringly. A nervous horse can be real trouble in the chutes and often as dangerous as a certified chute-fighter, since it is equally as unpredictable. With a chute-fighter, you may know what to expect, but a nervous horse reacts mostly from fear and will fight unpredictably. Chris quickly calmed this horse down and gently began easing the slack out of the latigos.

He looked up at the sound of clanging metal and saw the first cowboy make his bid for the title. It was a fair ride, but he had missed his mark: no score. Chris renewed his concentration, visualizing the entire ride—especially the spur-out. Just as he made the last tug on the latigo, the cowboy in chute two cracked out into the arena. Chris watched the ride as he tied off the loose ends of the leather latigos.

As the whistle sounded, Chris was pulling himself back out of the chute. He still had to get his chaps tightened up and his glove strapped on. The cowboy in chute three was ready to ride but was held back until the previous rider's horse was cleared from the arena. Chris reached around behind his legs and buckled up the straps to his chaps, then he went for his rosin bag. His glove was tucked into his belt, and Chris now pulled it loose and slipped it onto his riding hand. He jumped up onto the chute fence and patted rosin on his hand-hold on the rigging, then tapped a liberal amount onto his glove hand before tossing the rosin bag back toward his gear.

The rider in the chute ahead of Chris nodded his head and bolted into the arena. Chris was too busy now to watch the ride, sliding down onto his own horse and getting ready to make a bid for the crown. The cowboy slipped slightly out of position and was bucked off a second or two before the whistle, which meant Chris had even less time now than before. He ran his hand into the hand-hold and looked out into the arena just in time to see the previous rider's victorious steed being escorted out by the pick-up man.

"All right, cowboy, the judges are almost ready," he heard a voice call from the arena. Chris hadn't looked up, but he knew it was the chute boss. He pulled the fingers of his glove through the hand-hold, getting some slack in the tips. Then he closed his fist slightly and fed the slack over the top of the handle and into the palm of his hand. Thus bound up, he rotated his wrist a quarter turn, "setting" it into position. (This procedure is called a "finger tuck" and has since been outlawed due to the extreme danger of the rider becoming hung up.)

"Okay cowboy, everybody's ready ... nod your head."

Chris slid up onto the rigging as far as he possibly could, being very careful to keep his spurs out of the animal's neck or sides, then he pulled his hat down tight with his free hand. In his mind he was already two jumps into the arena with his spurs held tightly in the pocket of the neck, getting ready to start his spur-ride. He nodded his head.

The horse hestiated just a fraction of a second, but Chris waited for her to commit herself into the arena before he "put the metal to her." Then, just as her shoulder began to lean into the arena, he shot a solid spur-stroke into the pocket and held it there. She exploded, making her high-dive into the arena. If Chris hadn't had such a good grip with his spurs, surely he would have been jerked out of position. But his mark was true and held him tightly in place. On the second jump, he pulled back with his feet and dragged his spurs up nearly to his rigging, then settled into a smooth stroke. The mare cut back to the right in a short semi-circle and was almost back in front of the chutes by the time the whistle sounded.

Chris reached up with his free hand and pulled himself upright. As his spurs came out of her neck, the horse stopped bucking and took off on a dead run for the opposite end of the arena. The skillfull pick-up men, however, had already anticipated this and were moving in to cut her off, pulling up beside the bay on opposite sides. As one adroitly released the flank strap, the other positioned himself so Chris could reach around his waist and pull himself across and behind the pick-up man, vaulting safely away from the deadly hooves of his own wild mount. Once on the ground, Chris became aware of the cheering crowd and tossed them a bashful wave as he headed back for the chutes.

As he got to the fence, the next rider was turned into the arena, and Chris's moment of glory was over for the day. Witch Holman was to be the last man out, so Chris trotted over to his chute to give a word of encouragement to his friend.

A few minutes later, the first go-around was over in the barebacks, and Chris had won the round. He and Witch walked towards the stripping chutes to reclaim their riggings.

"You know, Chris," Witch began, "you ought to come up to Kaycee this summer, and you and me'll go down the road to some RCA shows."

Chris, stroking his chin thoughtfully, replied, "You know, Witch, I just might do that ... I just might."

Chris remembered passing through Kaycee during the regular high school season when he had rodeoed up that way. The youngsters all wore hats that looked two sizes too big, and even the youngest had a plug of tobacco tucked down in his lip. Kaycee was really what he had been expecting when they moved to Cheyenne: nothing but cowboys and cowgirls, ranchers and farmers—honest, hard-working people who had a solid grip on their lives and didn't need to "go find themselves," as so many of Chris' contemporaries spoke of doing. Chris knew who he was—and what he wanted—and the more he visualized it, the more he liked the idea of moving up to Kaycee now that he had graduated.

The next day, he cornered Witch before the rodeo and asked, "Hey, were you serious about me coming up to Kaycee next month?"

"Darn right I was, Chris," Holman replied.

"Well, where would we stay? I mean, when we aren't out of town rodeoing or something?"

"Just leave everything to me, partner. We can stay with some friends of mine," Witch replied with a grin as he slapped Chris on the back.

"Well, all right, Witch," he drawled, "but don't you be surprised when I show up on your doorstep."

"I'll be waiting for you, buddy, with my saddle packed and ready."

They moved over behind the chutes and, in the company of other roughstock riders, were soon back in the present, with the state championship resting on today's ride. Chris knew winning the first go-around yesterday had put him in pretty good shape. Even if he didn't win the round today, with a good showing he could still capture the average.

In rodeos with more than one head of stock, each time a contestant rides or ropes, it is called a go-around, or "go." The scores from these go-arounds are then tabulated and an average figured. The result is that, for a two-head rodeo, you'll have a first go-around winner, a second go-around winner and an average winner. The average winner at Cheyenne that year would be the new state champ, and that was what mattered most to these cowboys. Though they seldom talked numbers, any one of the boys in the top five could tell you exactly what he had to score and what the other leaders would have to score in order for them to win.

Chris decided his best course of action would be to do exactly what he always did: get on and "go ahead" with the best spur-ride he could possibly muster. He had found from experience he just wasn't any good at easing-up on a horse. For him, it was either all or nothing, and he would go for it all this time. His goal was to equal his first-round score, three points ahead of the nearest competitor, then hope no one beat him by more than three points.

When the dust settled that day, however, Chris had not only matched his previous score but exceeded it, winning the second go-around also, amassing an impressive average total, and thereby the state title.

John Forbes picked up the buckle in the saddlebronc riding and Witch Holman placed well in both the saddlebroncs and the bulls, taking home a fancy trophy saddle as the runner-up for the all-around title.

As the sun faded into the crimson sky, Witch shook Chris's hand and grinned. "Congratulations, you rascal. You made one heck of a fine ride today."

"Well, that was just today, Witch," Chris countered modestly. "When I come up there this summer, you'll be whipping the spurs off of me."

"You really serious about coming up to Kaycee, Chris?"

"You're darn right, I am," Chris replied. "My dad is moving again, and since I'm now a high-school graduate, I reckon it's time I set out on my own . . . and this seems to be the best way to go."

"All right!" Witched slapped his leg. "We're gonna get in some good times this summer, partner."

They got into their own cars and headed out. As he turned onto the blacktop, Chris could see Holman's taillights in his rearview mirror.

"I'll see you next month, Witch," he said to himself. "Kaycee . . . hot dang!"

Chapter 4

Born To Follow Rodeo

Faded old blue Wranglers, dusty cowboy hat,
A pair of scuffed up boots upon your feet.
Can of pork-n-beans that you opened with your knife,
It's not much, but it's all you've got to eat.
You think of what your daddy said, if your money should
*   run low,*
"Just call, I'll send you bus fare to come home."
But you're just too proud to take it, and home won't be the
*   same—*
Now you've had a taste of rodeo.

You set out on the road to seek your boyhood dream,
To satisfy that hunger in your soul.
You wouldn't turn back now—even if you could,
You were born to follow rodeo.

All your money's gone, 'cept a twenty-dollar bill.
And that's your fees to enter Old Cheyenne.
All that's in your favor is youth, and your try,
And a deep, gnawing, desperate need to win.
As you step out on the highway with your thumb up in the air,
In your mind a promise has been made:
If this way of life don't kill you,
And you don't starve to death,
You swear you'll be the champion someday.

Chris LeDoux (Wyoming Brand Music),
from **Life as a Rodeo Man**

Chris stood quietly in the empty living room of the LeDoux home in Cheyenne. It was finally beginning to sink in that soon he would truly be out on his own. Today the family was going to leave Wyoming to join Al in Nashville . . . all except Chris.

"Well, buddy," he said to himself, "this is what you've always wanted."

He heard the front door open and turned to see his mother walking back into the house.

"Did you make a last check around the house, Chris?" she asked.

"Yes, Ma'am, I did," he responded, trying not to stumble over the words. "I think you got it all."

Bonnie could sense his hesitation, and she placed her hand on his shoulder.

"Chris—," she began.

"Aw, Mom," he interrupted, "don't worry about me. I'll be just fine. Witch said he's already cleared it with Dot and Bunny Taylor for me to move in with them this summer. Why, he's been living with the Taylors all year while he finished up school."

"I know," she replied hesitantly, "and I'm sure they're real good folks . . . it's just that I'll miss you, son." He turned and gave her a hug, and she kissed him lightly on the cheek. "You be sure to write now, you hear?"

Chris's face exploded into a big grin. "Shoot, I might even call from time to time!"

With that, Bonnie turned and walked out, knowing that to stay any longer would surely bring forth the tears she had been struggling to hold back all this time.

Chris watched them drive away, then turned back toward the living room once again. He wasn't in a big hurry to get out on the road; it seemed as if the house didn't want to let go of him, and he was afraid to close that door for the last time. He knew when he did finally walk out, it would be the end of his childhood. He had come to Cheyenne a lanky young boy and was leaving a grown man. While it was the end of a chapter of his life, he realized that it marked the beginning of a new period as well.

He had accepted a rodeo scholarship at Casper College in Wyoming and figured to set the college rodeo circuit on fire in the fall, but for the next three months he and Witch Holman and John Forbes were going to buddy up and go down the road together to as many RCA rodeos as they could squeeze into the summer. He wasn't quite sure of what to expect when he got to Kaycee, except for what Witch had told him on the phone.

"Hey Chris, pack your gear and come on up," he had said a few days ago. "The Taylors have been like a mother and father to me all year while I've been going to school, and they've said you're welcome to stay with us for the summer."

"Well shoot, Witch, it sounds like you've got everything all figured out," Chris had replied. "I sold Comanche and bought an old clunker for a hundred bucks, so we'll have wheels to get to the rodeos."

"Great! When do you think you'll be here?"

"Well, Mom and the rest of the family are leaving Wednesday, so I guess I'll hang around until then, anyway . . . yeah, I'll be up Wednesday night sometime."

"Hey, there's a rodeo down in Grover, Colorado, this weekend. Do you want me to get us entered?" Witch had asked.

"You bet!" Chris had responded enthusiastically.

Slowly and deliberately Chris backed out the front door and pulled it shut behind him. He tested it once to make sure it was locked, then he turned and quickly walked away, never looking back.

"That's how it's going to be from here on in," Chris thought to himself. "No more looking back . . . just going forward all the time, and always moving toward that shiny gold buckle somewhere down the road."

A few days after arriving in Kaycee, Chris and Witch were packing up for their first RCA rodeo when John said, "Don't let me forget that guitar of mine, Chris."

"Okay," Chris responded absently, imagining a quiet evening around a campfire with their guitars out, singing cowboy songs and telling tall tales. In an hour the two men were on the road, heading into Kaycee for a few supplies before they started out in earnest on their trip.

"Hey Chris," Holman said. "Pull over at the Hole-in-the-Wall Bar. I've got a little errand to run—it'll just take a few minutes."

Chris did as he had been asked, and Witch bolted from the car, leaning in through the back window to grab his red Gibson guitar.

"Hey! What're you doing?" Chris called out as his partner vanished into the darkened interior of the bar.

In a few minutes Witch reappeared. At his side was a stranger, who now held the guitar. As they approached the car Chris got out and moved to the front of the vehicle to meet them.

"Chris, I'd like you to meet Dennis Elm," Witch said, sweeping his hand toward the stranger. "Dennis, this here is my rodeo partner, Chris LeDoux." The two shook hands, and Witch added, "Dennis is going to hold my guitar for me while we're down in Colorado ... and he spotted me fifty bucks till we get back."

They chatted idly for a few minutes, then the two climbed back into the car and waved to Dennis as they pulled out of the parking lot.

"You son of a gun!" Chris nearly shouted a few seconds later. "You hocked your guitar."

"I know, but I had to get my entry fees for Grover. Besides, I'll win that back and then some," he boasted proudly.

"And suppose you don't, hot shot," Chris chided good naturedly.

Witch just looked out the window at the passing scenery and replied quietly, "I will."

As it turned out, Witch did win the money back—plus a few dollars more—with a showing in the saddle bronc riding, so he managed to get his guitar back the very next day. Chris had drawn big white horse, and while he put in a respectable performance on the animal, he placed well out of the money. For his first-ever "pro" rodeo, however, he was quite pleased with himself.

"After all," he reasoned, "there were some real top hands here today: Les Gore, Jim Mihalek, and a whole slew of others who have already paid their dues and are genuine pros." Still, he knew he had been somewhat intimidated by those names on the entry list. Add to that the anxiety which he had already felt in coming to his first RCA rodeo and he was proud that he hadn't made a fool out of himself by bucking off or something equally embarrassing.

A couple days after the rodeo, Chris and Witch were talking about entering a few more upcoming shows, and the inevitable subject of money came up again. The little bit John had won had been used to redeem his guitar and pay for gas and food, so he was broke again, and Chris was getting down to his last few dollars.

"Well, we gotta come up with some money so's we can enter North Platte, Nebraska," Chris said.

"Well, if you'd have put some metal to that white bronc down in Grover, we just might have enough already," Witch teased, knowing they had both dreamed of winning big at Grover, thus making "stake" money for the rest of the summer. But now, it seemed, they were forced to examine other, less pleasant options—such as finding a job.

"Wait a minute," Holman exclaimed, sitting up quickly, "It's haying season, and my sister's husband is working on a ranch a few miles out. He can always use a hand putting up hay, and he usually pays a pretty fair wage."

"Great!" Chris shouted. "Give him a call and see if we can do it."

The next day, the boys drove out to the ranch, and after a casual lunch with Witch's sister and brother-in-law, they all retired to the porch to talk "hay." Having never done much of this type of work, Chris listened attentively to what was expected of him as a member of the team. After a few hours, Witch got up and strolled nonchalantly toward the door.

"Well, listen everyone, I've got to be getting back to town now," he said as he dug in his pockets for the car keys. Chris was confused. He had thought they were going to be staying on the ranch during their tenure here. He started to get up and walk out with Witch, who held up his hand to him. "Don't bother getting up, old buddy, I can see my own way out. I'll be back next week to pick you up."

Chris was stunned. It seemed everyone in the room was aware Witch wasn't going to be working there that week— everyone except Chris. Before he could register a complaint, Holman had slipped out the door, fired up the car, and was tearing off down the driveway toward the main road.

As the truth set in, Chris muttered to himself, "Well, you son-of-a-gun, you never had no intentions of gettin' no job. You just wanted *me* to get a job. You-son-of-a-gun."

The week went by very quickly, and Chris really enjoyed the hard work of stacking hay. The pay was pretty good, and he soon had enough of a grubstake to cover a few rodeos, so he bid farewell to Witch's in-laws and moved back in with the Taylors in Kaycee.

In the years to come, he would seldom let an opportunity slip by to razz Witch for having run out on him at the ranch. At the present time, however, the sting was still too fresh to talk about. Instead, Witch and Chris just talked rodeo and were soon making plans for North Platte.

They hitched a ride with Bill Dickson in his truck, with the three of them chipping in for gas. North Platte was a four-head rodeo, and when they pulled into the grounds, their first stop was at the rodeo secretary's office to check on how they had drawn for their first go-round. Chris was still studying the list when another cowboy noticed what Chris had drawn.

"I see you got Shiner," he stated.

"Yeah, you know him?" Chris asked.

"Well, I've been on him a couple of times." He turned his head to spit, then he finished, "He's a little strong."

"Hey, thanks a lot," Chris responded, thinking "I can handle him if he's just a *little* strong."

An hour later Chris lowered himself down onto Shiner and nodded his head. The horse ripped out like a freight train going downhill. Chris sank back a little and tried to get a good grip with his legs, but the bronc was too much for him; after a couple of jumps, he found himself spitting dirt. Shiner was so strong he didn't just politely buck him off—he fired the cowboy over his head and smashed him rudely, face first, into the arena dust.

"Shoot," Chris muttered to himself as he dusted off his pride, "if that's just a 'little bit strong,' what in the heck am I going to do if I draw something really rank?"

Behind the chutes a few minutes later, the same cowboy Chris had spoken to at the office came up behind him and patted him on the back.

"I told you he was a little strong, didn't I?" he said with a good-natured smile. It finally dawned on Chris that if someone told you a horse was "a little bit strong," he meant that it was going to rip your arm off when they opened up the gate.

"Boy, you sure did!" he replied, brushing off more of the dirt which clung tenaciously to his clothes. From that day forth he listened very carefully to what anyone had to say about "strong" horses.

Later that week, Chris drew up a National Finals Rodeo horse named Pretty Sox and scored high enough to win the go-around for that day. His other two rides were fairly unimpressive, but for all of his trouble he did come out financially ahead.

Next they headed down to Alliance, Nebraska, where neither Chris nor Witch won anything. It wasn't too upsetting for Chris, but Witch was tapped out. Chris would have loaned him whatever he needed, but Witch wouldn't hear of it. He made up the excuse he was needed back home in Kaycee for

some important work, and bid Chris and Bill Dickson farewell
to hitch a ride back home.

Meanwhile, Bill and Chris loaded up the truck and headed
for Kansas City. It was an exciting rodeo, and Chris even
managed to pocket some short-go money but didn't make it
into the finals.

When the show was over, Bill decided to keep going south,
while Chris wanted to turn back north. They parted company
in Kansas City, and Chris caught a ride with Jack Buschbom
to Boulder, Colorado.

At nineteen years of age, Chris was at that stage in many
young men's lives when they are highly influenced by what
others do and say. Chris was eager to learn from the "old-
timers," the twenty-five to forty-year-old cowboys who had
been making a living at rodeo for more than just a year or
two. He wanted to find out all about the life from someone
who would know firsthand. Jack Buschbom was just such a
person.

Jack Buschbom was the World's Champion Bareback Rider
in 1949, the year before Chris was born. He won the title again
in 1959 and 1960, and was in the top five from 1947 through
1962. He had rodeoed with the likes of Jim Shoulders, Casey
Tibbs, Bill Linderman, Deb Copenhaver and Freckles Brown,
among the many other notable champions of that era.

As they sped past the lonely wheat fields of Kansas toward
the majestic Rocky Mountains of Colorado, the car was filled
with the stories and advice Chris yearned to hear, told in a
manner only a former champion could tell. Jack gave Chris
a wealth of information and encouragement, and especially
warned him against switching to "those hard-handled riggings
Jim Houston has come up with ...." (Chris did eventually
go to a fiberglass or rawhide handle, but never one of metal.)
It was a magical time for the young cowboy, and he tried to
absorb all the words, hoping to tell them later to Witch, John
Forbes, and anyone else who would care to listen.

"The thing you want to do, Chris, is get around some of
the best. Just stick your thumbs down in your belt and walk

on over to where they hang out, just like you were supposed to be there. Then, whatever you do, don't open your mouth. First mistake a kid makes is trying to make-believe he's somethin' that he's not, and those guys will see through you in a second.''

Jack paused to look the young cowboy in the eye, then looked back at the road. ''The best way to learn, Chris, is to watch and listen to the top bareback riders, guys who are winning the championships, guys who are in the top fifteen—fellers liked that Young Clyde Vamvoras.

''There's no great secret to becoming a champ. It takes a lot of gettin' on, and lots of try. You have to use your head, too.

''Another thing: get to know the bucking horses—ask about them.''

There was a moment of silence as the words of the legendary cowboy were etched deeply into his memory, then Chris piped up, ''Did you ever get to ride that paint horse Cheyenne?''

A grin spread across Jack's face. ''You bet!'' he replied. ''There's probably been more money won on that horse than any other horse ever. He won't hardly even pull on you. He's so weak feelin' that you gotta really lay back and spur him. He's nice to ride.''

The stories just seemed to keep tumbling out, one right after the other. The ride took hours, but for Chris the time seemed to sweep past in just a few minutes. As the sun cast a pale glow across the snow-capped peaks of the Rockies, Chris and Jack pulled into the rodeo grounds at Boulder.

Later in the afternoon Chris discovered that, while neither he nor Jack were up for that night's performance, Clyde Vamvoras was. Clyde was in the lead for the championship in the bareback riding, and Chris wanted to watch him ride.

Seeing some friends out by the chutes, he strolled over to bid them hello. The next few hours seemed to drag by forever, but finally the evening came, and Chris found a spot behind the chutes where he could watch all of the action, both behind and in front of the gates. He had learned Clyde was probably going to be arriving just in the nick of time, as he was driving in from Cheyenne's afternoon performance.

The arena was cleared and groomed one last time for the grand entry, and still there was no sign of Vamvoras. Then, just as the horses came thundering down the alleyway, Chris noticed a commotion over by the back gate. Several cowboys with rigging bags were getting cleared by the gate guard to come into the grounds.

"Well, that must be them," Chris figured.

As the latecomers drew nearer, one of them ran ahead and pushed into the crowded area behind the chutes, looking for a horse.

"Here he is, Clyde, in number four," said the cowboy. One of the other cowboys just put up a hand, indicating he had heard. The last of the newcomers was carrying a saddlebronc saddle, so Chris knew the one with the uplifted arm must be Clyde.

Chris couldn't believe his eyes! The man leading the race for the championship, whom he had been looking forward to seeing all day, was sporting a three-day growth of beard, had a severe black eye and, from the way he was stumbling around, looked like he had had a few stiff drinks on the way over. Chris's image of the rider was shattered.

The other two cowboys helped Clyde get his rigging on his horse. Chris just stared at the spectacle open-mouthed, glad the crowd couldn't see this. Clyde climbed on and, half-hanging onto the gate, nodded his head. The next few seconds seemed an eternity as the bronc jerked the rider around unmercifully, as if sensing the condition he was in. Then suddenly, it was all over for Clyde. He was savagely thrown into the dirt and lay limp upon the ground. An ambulance was called in and carried him out of the arena like a fallen warrior.

"*That* is going to be the next World Champion?" was all Chris could think, shaking his head bitterly. He was terribly disillusioned. He would not find out until many months later that Clyde had been in four performances in the last three days and was severely injured in the Wild Horse Race at Cheyenne (where he had acquired the black eye) and was carried out there, as well. Instead of going on to the hospital, however, he had left the ambulance, grabbed his rigging bag, and headed for Boulder. Taking into account the punishment he had endured in the past few days, his condition at Boulder really didn't seem too far out of line.

Without knowing it, Chris had, in fact, witnessed the very thing which later won the World Championship for Clyde, and the championships for several years to come: his unconquerable and indomitable spirit of competition, that which drove him to actually exceed the physical limits his body could endure. He saw not a drunken slob, as he had thought, but rather a battered but unbeaten warrior, displaying an incredible amount of courage and fortitude, and a man well deserving of the crown he would later receive.

Chris didn't ride well the next night and caught a ride back to Kaycee. As the days passed, his disillusionment waned, and soon he could remember the gleam in Jack's eyes as he had talked during that drive to Boulder. It helped to revive his spirits somewhat. But there can be no denying that Chris was at an emotional low at this early point in his career. Nonetheless, he and Witch Holman and John Forbes all packed their gear and headed up to Tensleep, Wyoming, for a rodeo.

Every year on the Fourth of July, folks come down from the hills around Tensleep and have themselves a rodeo. It's the kind of wild-west fun you have to be a part of at least once in your lifetime to believe. There's dancing in the streets, parades, fights, pretty women, flashy young cowboys, and some fine rodeo action. This year, Chris drew up well in the first go-around and won second place for the day, so they all had a good time that night.

The next day, however, something just didn't quite settle into place for Chris. He hadn't been drinking the night before;

that just wasn't his style. But for some reason he just didn't have a lot of heart when he lowered himself down into the chutes. He nodded his head, and as the gate opened, he placed his spurs out over the breaks of the shoulders of the horse. But after that he sort of gave up. Those who watched say it appeared he just quit and fell off!

Chris knew he had quit, but he didn't think anyone else knew, so he was really surprised when he walked back behind the chutes and was approached by a veteran bareback rider whom he had met at Cody, Wyoming.

"I used to think you had some try," the cowboy began, "but you sure didn't today. You're not riding good at all. Maybe you're burned out and should quit for a year. Ya know, sometimes that's what it takes. You sure didn't have no try today, by golly, and you need to do something...."

"Give it up for a year? Is that what he'd said?" Chris asked himself as he watched the cowboy walk away. Chris toyed with a pebble with his boot as he thought, then came to a decision: he *had* given up today, but it was going to be the last time he would *ever* give up at a rodeo. In fact, he would ask the stock contractor for another horse to ride, just for a confidence builder.

Unfortunately the contractor told him there would be no extra horses that day, since all the contestants had shown up. Chris, again feeling despondent, sat down in the dirt behind the chutes as the rodeo wound down to its conclusion.

About half an hour later, with his head hung between his knees, he noticed a pair of worn-out old cowboy boots standing toe to toe with his own. He quickly looked up and stared into a weathered but kindly old Indian face which looked like it was covered in worn leather.

"I understand you're looking for a horse to get on," the Indian said without a smile.

"Yeah, that's right," Chris replied.

"Well, I got one," the Indian said quietly. Chris could see a sparkle in his eyes, and he knew whatever this old man had brought down, it would be a bucking fool! He was on his feet before he realized it, and getting his gear back on while the old man went to run up his horse.

Chris knew that if his promise never to quit was going to mean anything at all, then this had to be the best effort he had ever made, so he set himself to the task of getting psyched up for the ride. Witch Holman came over and started rigging up the horse while Chris paced back and forth behind the chutes, building a mental picture of the ride and getting a "feel" for the horse.

"Okay, Chris," Witch called from the chute, "rigging's all set, so any time you're ready, cowboy."

Chris climbed up onto the chute, lowered himself down onto the horse, shoved his hand into the hand-hold, cracked back on his wrist and nodded his head. As the gate clanged open, he lay back and started spurring. The horse exploded like a wild tornado, turning to the right in a tight, vicious circle, then back to the left. Chris knew the horse was spinning because he could see the clouds turning around above him.

"Stick 'em in, drag em' up, then fire 'em back down again" was all that was going through his mind. He could feel the writhing, surging animal beneath him, but was aware of his feet and the circling clouds overhead.

He could see a piece of the top section of bleachers, then the sky again, then the bleachers, then the sky—bleachers, sky, bleachers, down now to where some of the people were sitting, sky, clouds still spinning, people, bleachers, dirt, people, dirt, dirt, dirt. He was off and shaking his head, still trying to figure out what had happened. He looked at the horse and then he understood: his rigging had slipped over sideways and now hung almost under the horse. But he hadn't stopped spurring him at all, not until he was on the ground.

What remained of the crowd went completely wild over this exhibition ride, as did the cowboys behind the chutes who had seen it. Chris realized he must have ridden the bronc for fifteen or twenty seconds before he lost it. And he never gave up!

Proudly, he walked back towards the chute, where the veteran cowboy showed up again, the one who had chewed him out after his last ride.

"Now that's more like it," he beamed as he clapped Chris on the back. "That's what I call 'try'."

Tensleep, Wyoming, was a rodeo that would be forever etched into Chris's mind and heart. Of course every cowboy will suffer weak-hearted moments, and Chris was certainly no exception, but never would he slip as low as he had at Tensleep on his first ride that day, nor recover so completely as he had on the second.

Chapter 5

He Rides the Wild Horses

Just a rodeo drifter, he comes and he goes
Like a wild wind that blows in the night.
The highways and backroads are all that he knows,
And he'll be gone with the morning's gray light.
Like a blue norther howling, like the tumbleweeds blow,
There's no way to settle him down.
His spirit's as wild as the horses he rides,
His freedom he wears like a crown.

And he rides the wild horses—
The same blood flows through their veins.
Yes, he rides the wild horses—
And like the horses, he'll never be tamed.

He'll never be broke—he won't be tied down,
He'll never wear no man's brand.
He won't fit in with the nine-to-five crowd,
Movin's all he understands.

Chris LeDoux (Wyoming Brand Music)
from **He Rides the Wild Horses**

About twenty miles west of Kaycee, Wyoming, towering
some six hundred feet above the valley floor, stands ''the Red
Wall.'' The vivid orange and red cliffs are awe inspiring in
their majesty and beauty, as well as their historical significance;
in an apparently unbroken face is the infamous ''Hole-in-the-

Wall," which proved a nearly impregnable fortress for the bands of outlaws that used to roam the Wild West a hundred years ago.

In these same hills and valleys, several herds of wild and renegade horses still run. Having rekindled his resolve to become the World's Champion, Chris knew the key was to get on as many bucking horses as he possibly could, during the summer before college, to gain the seasoning needed to separate the novices from the "old hands." Chris, Witch and John felt those wild horses could provide just the ticket.

"We ought to go out to the Blue Creek Ranch and talk Curt Taylor into letting us gather some of those wild horses to practice on," suggested Witch. "We can haul the saddle horses up the slope of the mountain to where the horses are, then we'll run 'em down to the corrals at the ranch. From there we can take them on into Gosney's Arena."

"Heck, yeah!" responded Chris enthusiastically.

"Curt will probably want to ride a couple himself," said Forbes.

The three quickly agreed on the procedure and, after making arrangements with Curt Taylor, loaded up a livestock truck with the saddle horses and headed up the slope.

Finding the horses took very little effort, as the herds had taken to the high country during the hot summer months. Expert horesemen all, the three cowboys soon had a small herd rounded up and headed back down the mountain to the ranch. Mixed in with the purely wild horses were some that had been broken at one time and had either escaped or been turned loose again; these were somewhat more accustomed to the presence of men. So herd management was a little easier, but the cowboys quickly learned these former saddle horses were not at all eager to relinquish their freedom and were a constant source of antagonism.

That evening they backed the truck up to the corral and loaded ten of the healthiest horses for the trip back to Kaycee. By nightfall, the remainder of the herd had been turned loose.

The exhausted cowboys headed into town and unloaded the horses at the arena, after which they went home for a good night's rest.

At first light, Chris and Witch were up and dressed, tossing their riding gear together in preparation for a long day of roughstock riding. Ten broncs between the three of them, plus Curt Taylor, would be plenty of practice—if they were physically able to withstand that much punishment. They had all agreed they were anxious to try. John Forbes was already at the arena when Chris and Witch arrived.

"All these horses to be rode and you two pick today to sleep in," he teased them playfully.

"What the heck are you talking about?" Chris countered. "We were down here hours ago waiting for you to show up."

"Yeah, that's right," Witch joined in. "We've already run the herd through once, then we went and ate breakfast."

"Oh, sure," Forbes responded with a grin. "I suppose that explains why your britches are still clean and purty, and why, when I stopped at the cafe for a cup of coffee a while ago, the waitress asked me where you two were hiding out."

"All right, all right, you've caught us, boss," Chris sighed dramatically. "Here it is, fully an hour after sun up, and we're just now showing up. I suppose you'll just have to take it out of our pay."

The three had a good laugh as they laid out their gear behind the chutes. Curt had arrived a few minutes earlier and was saddling a horse that he could use for pick-up when he wasn't riding a bronc himself. With only the four of them, it would be a slow process, since it took one rider, one gate man and a flank man for each ride, plus the pick-up man. Afterward the horse had to be herded out of the arena and into the stripping chute—a considerable chore with some of those wild horses—and the next horse run up.

After a few hours, they did pick up a little help from some of the local cowboys, who had turned out to see what all the excitement was about down at the usually quiet arena. As payment for their services, the locals were allowed to mount one of the broncs out from time to time. They soon found they had plenty of horses, even for seasoned old permit-holders like themselves, so they didn't really mind sharing a few with the others.

By the time they broke for lunch, they had all been out on four head a piece and were beginning to feel the physical effects of the hours of punishment.

"Man, that son-of-a-gun really twisted my elbow on that last ride," Witch said to no one in particular as they sat in the café eating their lunch.

"Yeah, I thought he was gonna take you right through that fence, Witch," John responded. "And what about that buckskin that fell down with you, Chris?"

"Shoot," Chris replied, shaking his head, "I thought I was a goner. If that son-of-a-buck had rolled left, it would have been all over."

"All in all, this's a pretty even bunch so far, though," Witch added.

"Yeah, I'd say we picked a pretty good lot, all right," answered John.

"But, we're only half way home, fellers—and I don't know about you, but my hand is already gettin' kind of tender," Chris contributed.

"Maybe so, Chris, but with Rapid City coming up in a few days, we need all the practice we can get," John pointed out.

They all agreed, and after finishing their lunch and feeling somewhat refreshed, they eagerly set out for the arena to complete the task at hand. By sundown, however, they had all learned another very valuable lesson: even though it's true every young cowboy should get on as many head as he possibly can, he shouldn't try to do it all in one day! All three of the riders ended up with some pretty serious aches and pains, which served to negate any possible gains they might have realized in their marathon session.

Chris, in particular, had torn the flesh from the palm of his riding hand, which was a serious problem; not only because

of the pain he would experience in his next ride, but because
he would tear the wound open again each time he rode, making for a very long recovery period if he didn't take some time
off.

But taking time off the circuit was the furthest thing from
the boys' minds. The next weekend they were all loaded up
and headed out for Rapid City, South Dakota. Chris had
decided he was ready for the pros, and he intended to prove
it at Rapid City.

During the short lull between rodeos, Chris had made a pair
of gold metallic chaps with silver trim, and he had spray-
painted a pair of boots a shiny silver to match. It was a com-
bination that would definitely leave an impression on anyone
who happened to be at the rodeo, and since Rapid City was
a four-head rodeo, there would be plenty of chances for folks
to see this bizarre outfit. Even those who knew Chris well,
such as Holman and Forbes, tended to keep their distance once
he donned his shimmering accoutrements. The top hands, such
as Jimmy Ivory, wondered, "Just who in the heck is this son-
of-a-buck from Wyoming with silver boots and gold chaps?"
Chris didn't let them wonder for long, however, as he rode
three of his four horses into the money and finished third in
the average.

"Hey, Chris, maybe now you can afford to buy you some
new chaps," someone said. Chris just let the remarks slide past
with a chuckle, for the chaps had done what he had intended:
they had gotten him noticed. And to top it all off, he was standing in the pay line, while some of the best "looking" cowboys
were opening a cold can of pork-n-beans for supper.

Actually, the idea for the flamboyant attire was based on
sound thinking. Chris had heard a few of the old timers talking about how poorly lit some of the arenas were, and how
difficult it was for the judges to watch a rider's feet at night.
At one such arena, Chris noticed a cowboy who had used white
athletic tape to repair a torn boot. The boot had been wrapped
with the tape, and when the cowboy bucked out into the dim

ly lit arena, the taped boot really stood out well. Chris figured the silver spray paint would work even better, and when he came upon the material for the gold chaps it just seemed a natural match-up. Soon, though, he decided the idea was still somewhat ahead of its time, and he retired the outfit.

During his first summer after graduation, the nineteen-year-old LeDoux managed to enter quite a few RCA rodeos, and by the end of the summer he had developed a pretty good name for himself as a rookie. When he wasn't riding at a regular rodeo or bucking out on some freshly rounded-up wild horses, he could usually be found at the Cody Nightly Rodeo in Cody, Wyoming. Cody always provided some challenging stock and plenty of excitement for young cowboys like Chris and his friends.

One night at the Cody Rodeo, Witch Holman and a friend named Jim Smith had had enough of bronc riding and decided to have a few beers to help them relax. Chris stayed out behind the chutes with some of the other cowboys, not being much of a drinker himself, and hardly noticed that Jim and John had left. But if he hadn't been aware of their departure, he was certainly aware of their return.

In the short time they had been gone, the two cowboys had imbibed enough of the "relaxing" beer to be feeling absolutely no pain. Upon returning to the arena, they decided to appoint themselves coaches to the numerous amateur bronc riders who were in and behind the chutes.

Usually, when one of the older, more experienced hands chooses to share a few words of wisdom with the younger contestants, his ideas are eagerly listened to, but when the advice is being offered quite loudly by a young drunk staggering around the arena like a twice-roped steer, his words usually are not warmly received. Such was the case when John and Jim made their re-entry to Cody that night.

"Don' be afraid," John stammered, "git down on 'em an' nod yer head." He motioned with his arm for one young rider to get down into the chute and get set on the horse.

Jim had moved over to the side of the arena and was watching the spectacle Holman was making of himself. Being nearly as drunk himself, he could only giggle at John's behavior. Behind the chutes, Chris had seen the two come into the arena together but hadn't really paid much attention to what they had been up to since—until John started shouting at the young rider in chute two.

"What're you waiting for, cowboy?" he started. "Take your lead an' nod your face!" He emphasized the last part of his comment by raising his "rein" hand in the air in a tight fist and shaking his head up and down.

"Hey, you!" boomed a voice from the back of the arena. "Leave 'at kid alone. He'll come out when he's ready." It was the chute boss, coming back from a short break. He was a massive man, standing six-foot-four and weighing in at around two-seventy, and he was getting madder by the minute.

John turned to face his adversary. Seeing the sheer bulk of the man, he pulled his 135-pound frame up to its fullest, then decided he wasn't quite *that* drunk. He slowly weaved his way over to the side of the arena, where Jim was leaning up against the fence, doubled over with laughter.

He tried hard to look tough, but seeing his friend, Witch broke out laughing as well. The chute boss had reached the center of the arena, planted his feet squarely and crossed his arms, just watching the drunken cowboys with a scowl on his face.

Suddenly the gate burst open, and the young puncher in chute two made his bid for the jackpot. The sparse crowd of friends, wives and girlfriends did their best to raise a cheer, but the cowboy took a dive just seconds before the whistle, dashing his hopes and his pride into the dust.

Picking himself up and brushing off the dirt, the cowboy was walking back to the chutes when Witch shouted to him, "I told you not to be afraid of him—you gotta work that son-of-a-buck, not let him work you."

The words stung the young cowboy like buckshot, and as he walked straight to the gate, his back stiffened visibly at the taunting remark. The chute boss watched the whole thing, then pointed a stubby finger at John. "One more word out of you and I'm gonna toss you outta here, cowboy. You got that?"

John clapped both of his hands over his mouth dramatically and sat down quickly. The chute boss turned back to his job at the gates, confident the matter had been settled.

Chris, meanwhile, still engrossed behind the chutes, had been paying very little attention to the goings-on out front. One of the young riders he had been helping now settled himself down into chute four and began placing his feet into the stirrups of the saddlebronc saddle. Chris walked out the gate into the arena, where he could more closely observe his protegé and offer a hand, if needed, to the gate crew.

After just a few minutes, the cowboy slid into position, raised his rein hand into the air, and nodded his head. The gate cracked open.

Without thinking, Witch jumped up, threw a fist into the air and hollered, "Charge, kid, charge!"

Chris did not see the scarlet-faced chute boss turn and storm off in the direction of Witch and Jim; he was too busy watching the rider and his mount. But by the time the novice was safely on the ground, there was quite a commotion in front of the stands. The chute boss had grabbed John by the throat and was lifting him out into the arena, all the while cussing and hollering at him.

"I told you to shut your mouth, didn't I, smart guy?" he roared as he rattled and shook John like a rag doll. Finally, several people pulled the two apart, and while John struggled to regain his breath, a small crowd gathered around. Seeing the altercation, Chris trotted over to see what was going on— then he saw John and realized what had happened. The chute boss was still yelling and shaking his fist at Witch when Chris shouldered his way through the gathering.

"What'd he do?" he asked quietly, with his thumbs tucked into his belt.

The big man stopped in mid-sentence and turned to Chris. "Listen," he shouted, red-faced. "You shut up. I'm not talking to you." Then he turned back toward John, but before he could utter another word, Chris spoke quietly again.

"Look, all I want to know is what he did," Chris said, crossing his arms as he spoke.

Without warning, the big man drew back and, with his left fist cocked, threw a wild roundhouse punch in Chris's general direction. Fortunately for Chris, he missed.

Not being much of a fighter, Chris didn't really know what to do, but he figured if he didn't hit the man hard and fast, he would be in serious trouble with the next blow. So he stepped into the man and unleashed a quick right jab to the belly, followed by a left to the face.

Chris hadn't been in very many fights, but he had pulled on a lot of riggings with his left hand, so there was tremendous power in that arm, of which Chris was unaware. The punch exploded just above the chute boss's right eye. The big man staggered backwards from the blow and a trickle of blood began flowing down his cheek.

Shaking his head, the big man retaliated by charging his smaller opponent, catching Chris in the chest with his head and gripping him in a bear hug. Chris, with both hands free, began pummeling the face of the big man, and they waltzed around in front of the stand in that fashion for a few seconds before the crowd finally pulled them apart.

Chris's shirt had been torn, but he was relatively unhurt. The chute boss, on the other hand, had taken several powerful punches to his face, which was now cut and bruised. There were no serious injuries, however, and after glaring at Chris for a few seconds, the big man pushed his way through the crowd and out the back gates toward the barn and outbuildings. The crowd quickly dispersed, with contestants moving back behind the chutes and spectators moving back up into the stands. Some of the hired hands began moving the roping box barriers out of the way in preparation for the steer wrestling, which would be the next event.

Chris walked out in front to get a drink of water, and John and Jim headed out back to the pick-up truck for a couple more beers. They were tucked quietly into the darkened cab of the truck, talking about the fight and sipping on a beer, when the chute boss walked right in front of the truck, not seeing the boys.

As it happened, there was a water spigot in front of the truck, and the big man had taken off his shirt and was now wetting it so he could mop up his face. Witch and Jim sat perfectly still for a few seconds, looking at each other mischievously. Then John rolled his window down just a crack, and said, "What's the mater, hoss? That pup get the better of you?" Then he rolled up the window quickly.

Startled, the large man straightened up and squinted to see into the cab of the truck. When he recognized Witch, he ran to the side of the truck and tried to open the door.

"Open up, you little squirrel," he shouted as he banged on the window with his huge fist. John just raised his can of beer in toast and smiled at the man through the glass. Jim rolled down his window, on the safe side of the truck, and hollered "You'd better be careful, or we'll go get our buddy again."

This outraged the man and he started shaking the truck, but even he wasn't big enough to do any real damage. Frustrated, he grabbed his shirt and stormed back into the arena, madder than a hornet.

Meanwhile Chris had returned from getting a drink and was leaning against the fence, watching the bulldoggers work their event, when he heard the chute boss bellowing in his direction. Not aware of the recent antagonism, Chris was surprised to see the red-faced monster storming towards him.

"Oh, Lordy," he thought. "Here we go again."

When he came within a few feet of Chris, the big man stopped short. Still holding his shirt in his right hand, he pointed his left thumb at Chris. "Let's go outside and finish this thing, cowboy," he said with a raised eyebrow.

"Well, shoot," Chris said with a slight smile. "It's finished, as far as I'm concerned."

The man stood for a second, then rocked back on his heels. "Well, all right, but I don't want to hear about you braggin' around how you got the best of me tonight, or I'll hunt you up . . . then we'll see what happens." He turned slowly and walked out the back gate to finish cleaning up.

Chris decided it was time to go check up on Jim and Witch, and find out just what had happened. They were still locked in the cab of the truck, giggling like a couple of maniacs, when Chris pounded on the window. "All right, you yahoos," he said. "Open up. You got some explaining to do."

In the morning, Chris and Witch emptied out their pockets at the local cafe after breakfast.

"Well, by the time we pay for breakfast, put gas in the car, and buy a can of snuff, we ain't gonna have much over twenty dollars left," John mused.

"That'll be enough," Chris said confidently.

"Enough?" asked John curiously. "Enough for what?"

"I got me a sure fire way to pick up a few dollars on the way home," responded Chris slyly.

"Oh no, not again." Holman objected, holding up his hands in protest.

"Wait a minute, Witch, you ain't heard me out yet," defended Chris. This'll be great."

"All right, hot shot," replied Witch, straightening himself up in his seat. "Let's hear it."

Chris reached into his pocket and pulled out a folded piece of paper. Carefully unfolding it, he slid it across the table. John cocked his head around to read the poster.

"Okay, so they're having a junior steer-riding jackpot," said John, unimpressed by what he had seen. "Big deal."

"It says 'ages nine to nineteen'," said Chris expectantly. When he got no response from John, he continued, "Don't you get it? I'm nineteen, you idiot."

John's mouth dropped open, and he crossed his arms. "Naw, you're not seriously considering..."

"Sure I am. Think how easy it'll be winning that deal," Chris interrupted. "Why, it'll be like taking candy from a bunch of babies."

John started grinning and clapped Chris on the shoulder. "I gotta hand it to you, old buddy," Witch said, raising his juice glass in a mock toast. "I think you got a winner this time."

"What'd I tell you?" Chris answered, joining in the toast.

Shortly after noon, they arrived at the rodeo grounds and paid their twenty-dollar fee for Chris's entry into the steer-riding event. Walking back to the truck, they passed a huge cowboy walking a few feet away.

"Uh oh," John muttered, recognizing the chute boss from the night before.

Chris looked up quickly and caught the man eye to eye. They both stopped in their tracks, just a few feet apart. John walked a little further, just to get out of range, then turned to face the two.

The chute boss thrust out his huge right hand and a smile rippled across his face. "For a little feller, you pack a pretty mean punch, friend," he said sincerely.

Chris accepted the proffered hand, shook it firmly, and said, "Thanks. I'm just glad you didn't decide to kill me or something."

The big man rocked back with a hearty laugh. The tension broken, Chris and Witch chuckled, too. Then the man straightened up, and his face went completely blank. "Naw, it's *him* I'm gonna kill," he said pointing at Witch.

Witch choked on his laughter and reached for his throat, to protect it from the expected grip. Then the big man thrust out a paw toward him and said, "Just kidding, little buddy. Put 'er there."

"Hey, look," Witch offered apologetically, accepting the handshake, "I'm really sorry about last night ... I mean, we were *some* kind of drunk."

"Don't worry about it," said the big man. "Just don't let it happen again, right?" Witch shook his head, and they all parted friends.

A few hours later, after all of the younger age groups had had their turns, the senior division was called behind the chutes. Chris and Witch grabbed their gear and started across the arena toward the bucking chutes.

"Now listen," Chris began, "take that broom there, and when they open up the gate, you smack that son-of-a-gun right upside the head so's he'll turn back into a spin. We can't win no money if he just runs off across the arena."

"Yeah, yeah," Witch moaned, "I got it. Piece of cake, right?"

Chris nodded, then they picked out his steer and began rigging it up. There were quite a few other seniors in the division, but none quite so "senior" as Chris. He figured the nearest competitor to his own age would be about fifteen years old. He chuckled to himself.

Utilizing all the technique he had acquired over the years in bull riding, Chris lowered himself down on his steer and set up for the ride. Witch climbed up onto the gate and pulled the tail of Chris's bull rope, cinching Chris's hand tightly into position. Chris took the tail of the rope and wrapped it securely around his waist. "Now don't forget to smack him with that broom," he said.

"No problem," Witch replied, jumping down from the gate and picking up the broom from where he had left it.

The judges moved into place, and the chute help readied the gate. Chris nodded his head.

The steer, frightened out of its wits, bolted out of the chute at a dead run, throwing Chris back just a bit. Witch drew back, with all of the gusto he could manage, and swung the broom at the steer's head. The steer, saw it coming and, as nimbly as a prizefighter, ducked to one side and spun sharply around in a tight little circle—exactly what Chris had wanted him to do.

It was a shame Chris didn't get to see the spin, for when the steer made his move, it threw Chris soundly into the dirt, face first.

As the steer trotted off across the arena, Chris pulled himself to his knees and watched it go, not believing what had just happened. Witch, who had retrieved the bull rope, tossed it down just in front of Chris.

"Got any more bright ideas, hot shot?" John asked.

Chapter 6

Bareback Jack

When I was just a very young lad,
I walked up and I told my dad,
"A bareback rider's what I want to be,
I want the whole world to know about me.
In the rodeo arena I'll make my stand,
I wanna be known as a rodeo man."

The years of boyhood now have passed,
It didn't take long, I learned the tricks real fast.
Now I'm goin' down the road with my rodeo gear,
And I hope to make the Finals in just a few years.
When my chance comes I'll give it a whirl
And try to win the championship of the world.

I'll come flying from the chute with my spurs up high,
Chaps and boots reachin' for the sky.
Spurrin' wild, with my head thrown back,
You'll ask, "Who's that?", well that's Bareback Jack.

Here I am, I'm a-layin' in bed,
The son-of-a-buck jumped onto my head.
I'm laying here dying, and a-hurtin' real bad,
Now I wish I'd listened to my old dad
When he said, "Son, you'd better quit foolin' around,
"You're gonna get your guts stomped into the ground.

You'll come flying from the chute with your tail up
  high,

That old bucking horse will throw you in the sky.
And when you come down, you're gonna break your back,
And we'll all know you as 'Old Crippled-up Jack'
In a wheelchair, with a broken back."

Chris LeDoux (Wyoming Brand Music),
from **Rodeo Songs**

The rodeo season at Casper College was broken up into two segments: a short series in the fall and a longer set in the spring, with the finals in early summer.

The first big rodeo of the fall season was in Ft. Collins, Colorado. Chris, along with most of the other members of the rodeo team, had entered several events. Other members of the team that year included Tommy Joe "T.J." Walter, reigning High School All-Around Champion; Jack Ikes, former High School Bareback Champion; Keith Maddox, top bull rider and bareback rider; and several other notable contestants.

At Ft. Collins, Chris drew a horse named Satan's Sister in the saddlebronc riding that, at the time, was considered the scourge of the college rodeo circuit. Somehow, Chris managed to get by the horse and took first place for his efforts. In the bareback riding he placed in the money, and in the bull riding he was thrown off by a fairly rank bovine.

Chris was beginning to notice that, while he still enjoyed the bull riding, he seemed to be slipping farther behind in the skills required to be competitive at the event. As he got better at riding bucking horses, it became more of a natural reflex, rather than something he had to think about doing. But this same reflex which made him excel with horses actually handicapped him in the bull riding, which requires totally different reactions; he had to really concentrate on what he was doing on a bull, and consequently, it became a lot less fun.

Whatever his shortcomings in the bull riding, he was still a top "broncstomper" and welcomed into the college rodeo

team as "one of the gang." Chris, knowing T.J., Jack and
Keith to be somewhat wilder than himself, never really did
fit in, but they had some good times together. In the late fall,
one of the boys rented a house in Casper, and they decided
to have a party.

Not much of a drinker, Chris decided to bring along his
guitar and get his kicks on Copenhagen and music, while everyone else did their best to empty a keg of beer they had on ice
in the bathtub. Several other people had brought along in-
struments, amplifiers and microphones, and before long they
had a first-class stage area set up in the living room. Chris
planted himself in front of the equipment, guitar in hand, and
began to belt out some old favorites like "Johnny B. Goode"
and "I've Got a Tiger by the Tail." During the course of the
evening, other musicians joined him from time to time, and
they all had a lot of fun. As time wore on, however, the party
seemed to get louder and louder, so the musicians kept adjusting their volume accordingly. Before they knew it, the
neighbors were complaining.

Chris was enthusiastically belting out another tune when
suddenly everyone in the room bolted toward the front door.
At first he thought the jam-up was a direct response to his
music. "Shoot, I must be playing terrible to drive them all
outside like that," he thought.

Then he noticed two uniformed police officers following
behind the mass and ineffectually trying to round it up. Everyone made it out the door to freedom just as the officers entered
the living room. Chris just kept right on playing.

Satisfied with having ended the party, the policemen elected
not to pursue the fugitives. One of the cops turned to Chris
and held up his hand. "Shut 'er down, son," he said kindly.
"The party's over."

Chris shut down all of the equipment and carried his guitar
back to the dorm. Still feeling pretty good from the party,
he couldn't just go to bed, so he pulled his guitar back out
and began to strum a few chords. As he played, he got to
thinking about rodeo, and life as a bareback rider. Soon, a

song began to form in his head. He ran out and grabbed an old paper bag and a pencil and scratched out the words and tune to "Bareback Jack," his first rodeo song.

After finishing the short fall rodeo season, Chris and several other rodeo team members were anxious to get on some roughstock. Often, they would bolt down a quick supper at the dorm, since it was already paid for, and drive down to a covered arena in Laramie, where there was usually a practice buck-out or small jackpot for the boys to enter. Then they would drive back to Casper for a short night's sleep before school began the next morning.

In addition to the roughstock, Chris still liked to jump on a bale of hay as often as he could, and once he even sneaked a bale up to his dorm room. That didn't last for very long, however, as the dorm mother soon caught on and insisted it would be too much of a fire hazard for Chris to keep. Reluctantly, Chris hauled it back out again.

After a successful summer on his RCA permit, Chris received his card from the RCA, making him a full member of the Association. During the short fall college season, he hadn't really had much opportunity to use the new status by entering an RCA rodeo, but in the winter, he got a real craving for warmer weather and another rodeo. He decided to kill two birds with one stone: he would enter an RCA rodeo in Amarillo, Texas.

Chris and a photographer friend named Dan Hubble, who had also expressed an interest in going to Amarillo, began saving up their money for the trip. As neither of them was working, they soon realized it was going to be very tight.

To cut expenses, they would start saving up all the food they could scavenge from the cafeteria. That way, they would only have to spend money on gas and entry fees—or an occasional game of pool.

It was quite a sight to watch Chris and Dan turn every meal into a "Chip-n-Dale" cartoon; they barely ate any of their own food, instead stashing anything they could into a bag to carry back to their dorm rooms. They were especially adept at procuring those little, individual-sized boxes of cereal, but they also stockpiled crackers, jellies, butter, apples and oranges. Often, after dinner, they would take non-perishable handouts from their friends' plates. Soon they had constructed a couple of complete loaves of bread, a few slices at a time. By the end of two weeks, they had amassed several full shopping bags of food. With their scavenged provisions supplemented by a jar of store-bought peanut butter, they began loading up Chris's old '59 Ford.

"Doggone, it sure feels good to be out on the road again, don't it, Dan?" Chris asked as he turned out onto the main highway.

"Darn sure," replied the photographer with a shake of the head. "I was really gettin' antsy in that dorm all the time."

"Yeah, me too," responded Chris. "Hey, listen. There's a big rodeo going on down in Denver right now. Why don't we stop by there on the way to Texas and rub shoulders with some of the big boys?"

"Why not?" Dan replied with a grin. "It's right on the way, ain't it?"

Chris nodded, and they motored on towards Denver. They arrived in the early evening and headed straight for the Mayflower Hotel, where they knew all of the action would be taking place. There were cowboys and cowgirls everywhere.

The awards for the reigning World's Champions, by tradition, were presented at Denver, in conjunction with the big rodeo, and this ceremony had taken place just a few hours before Chris and Dan arrived at the Mayflower. The liquor had begun to flow almost immediately, and by the time Chris and Dan got there, the party was already in full swing.

Clyde Vamvoras, who had received the Gold Buckle in the bareback riding, was playing pool with some friends and feeling no pain. He was gnawing on a side of raw pork, and hacking and spitting on the floor.

"I am the Champ!" he hollered for all the world to hear, raising his drink into the air as a toast.

A roar of approval went out from those around the room, all cheering for their friend in his hour of glory. Clyde had earned this party, as had all the other champions scattered throughout the hotel, each celebrating and reflecting on the past season in his own way. Chris stuck a wad of Copenhagen in his lip and joined in the fun. It was a wild night, to say the least, and Chris and Dan eventually ended up on the floor of someone's room, getting a short bit of sleep before they continued on their journey to Texas the following morning.

The two cowboys arrived in Amarillo in the middle of a rainstorm early the following morning and parked the car at the rodeo grounds. Exhausted from their trip, they stretched out on the seats of the old Ford and slept for a couple of hours. When they woke up, they treated themselves to a breakfast of peanut-butter-and-Cocoa-Crispies sandwiches. Afterwards, they headed towards downtown Amarillo to look for a cheap place to spend the night. They found the Ross Hotel.

At that time, the Ross Hotel charged two dollars per night for a room with a single bed and a shower at the end of the hall. Chris and Dan forked over a buck apiece and moved their groceries and gear into their room. It wasn't much, but it would do in a pinch—and this was about as tight a pinch as they had ever been in.

The room cost less than what they had figured, so they celebrated by splurging the difference on their only hot meal of the trip: two "double super-duper, half-cooked burgers, and a side of grease-soaked french fries."* After eating, they headed on down to the rodeo grounds to get ready for that night's performance.

Chris drew a horse called Copeland in the first go-around. After a short ride on this very strong horse, he found himself airborne. The next night, on his second draw, he didn't fare much better; spurring out above the horse's neck, Chris's

---

*From *Fourth of July Rodeos,* Chris LeDoux (Wyoming Brand Music).

balance was so far off he had to "double grab," or reach up with his free hand and grab the rigging, to keep from being thrown off. The resulting no-score dashed his hopes of returning to Casper with a little extra cash in his pocket.

Dan had managed to sell a few pictures, so they didn't end up totally broke, but if they had driven into town like gangbusters, they were going out like whipped pups. They had had enough of moldy bread and stale crackers and peanut butter, plus the added humiliation of driving hundreds of miles for two "goose-eggs" for Chris.

As Dan pulled out onto the highway, Chris reached into the back seat for his guitar and began playing "Bareback Jack." Soon, their spirits were up again; they were really glad to be headed back home.

They had to stop in Cheyenne and borrow five dollars from an old friend for gas; some time later, they pulled into Casper without a dime between them. Looking back over the whole experience, Chris was glad he had gone, but at the same time was never happier to see that tired old dorm room.

He spent the rest of the winter playing cards, writing songs and, for the most part, relaxing in his dorm room. Of course, the college had a few practice horses, and Chris spent quite a bit of time down at the arena with the other team members, but most of the horses weren't much to ride. Usually, they would just scatter and run out of the bucking chutes. Chris started to fall into a slump and resolved to work even harder on the hay bales and such, but he felt part of his problem lay in the lack of good, sound bucking stock on which to practice.

There were also a few good horses in the college string, and the cowboys always raced for first chance at these, the slowpokes getting stuck with the "dinks." Chris decided if he was to break his slump, he was going to have to avoid the dinks altogether, so if he wasn't quick enough to get a good mount, he'd just pack his gear and head back to the dorm. This action led to problems between himself and the rodeo coach,

Dale Stiles, who insisted that all the cowboys get on a horse, good or bad.

"Put your riggin' on that bay, Chris," Stiles said one night.

"Naw. Heck, he'd just run off anyway," Chris responded. "I'm just gonna go get on a bale of hay and practice my spur lick."

"I've been watching you, LeDoux," the coach continued, "and the way you've been riding, you'd best get on anything that has four feet and a flank strap, pal."

"But I'm not learning anything on these runners," Chris protested. "I need something that'll buck."

"You don't get no choice at a rodeo," the coach pressed. "Besides, these broncs still have a little buck in 'em if you start 'em just right."

Sometimes the coach would have his way and Chris would get on one, and sometimes he would just walk away. But the friction was bad enough between him and Stiles nearly to get Chris booted off of the team; that is, until the spring season started, when he broke out of his slump and began winning rodeos.

He won the bareback riding at Pueblo, Colorado, taking first in both go-arounds and the average; he won at Lamar and at Casper, and placed well at several others. As the summer drew near, Chris had won the regional college title for the barebacks.

As in the fall, Chris had started out in the spring entering all three roughstock events—bulls, bares and broncs—but was still having serious problems with the bull riding. Finally, at one of the early spring rodeos, Chris watched a friend get mauled and nearly killed by a bull. As they carried the hapless rider away, Chris heard one of the ambulance attendants remark that he didn't think he'd ever be "right in the head" again. It was a sobering experience.

Young rodeo cowboys often have the feeling that they alone are protected from serious injury by some mysterious power. As the years go by, if they are lucky and avoid injury, that feeling just grows stronger. Then, one day they will see a rider they really admire go down hurt, and especially if he is someone they know to be a better rider than themselves, they realize their own mortality; they know down deep inside it really could happen to *them* just as easily.

Rodeo cowboys face death and injury every day, but they are highly skilled athletes who have, for the most part, a great deal of experience and schooling in their events. All this reduces the chances of serious injury. By learning the proper safety techniques from other competitors, and especially from schools and clinics, these cowboys can tilt the odds in their favor.

Seeing his friend on the stretcher really made Chris start to think about his own bull riding. He wasn't doing very well at it, although he did enjoy it. The real problem was he didn't have any instincts for it. The bareback riding seemed to come automatically—he would just fall back and go to spurring— but with the bulls he had to calculate every move. There were no reactions, and for him, it didn't seem to be getting any better. Some people are quite capable of learning and mastering both events, but Chris found the odds were no longer in his favor. He made a very tough decision that day: he pulled out his knife and cut his bull rope in half. It was not an act of fear, but rather one of pure logic. Now he was free to concentrate fully on the barebacks and saddlebroncs for which he seemed to have a knack, and not worry about a senseless injury in an event that didn't hold very promising odds for him.

Early in June, the National College Finals Rodeo was held in Sacramento, California. Chris, Keith Pollet, Phil Wood, and Delane Nixon packed up and headed out in one of the boys' truck/camper rigs. To make the trip more worthwhile, they decided to enter an RCA rodeo at Lehi, Utah, on the way to California.

When they pulled into Lehi, it didn't take long to find out a lot of other Sacramento-bound college riders had the same idea. It was a regular cowboy Ft. Lauderdale. There were women and parties everywhere, and Chris and his friends soon found themselves right in the thick of things. It turned out to be a very late night for the boys, and several of them woke with throbbing heads in the morning. Of course, Chris still didn't drink much, but he had had his share of the carousing and was not feeling much better than anyone else. They ended up staying in bed for most of the day.

That night Chris had drawn a horse named Three Below, a yellow horse with a lot of power. Chris slipped down into the chutes as the cowboy in front of him was nodding his head. LeDoux ran his hand into his rigging and cracked back on his wrist. The horse pawed the ground nervously and bolted into the gate a few times. Chris placed his feet on the rails, sitting astride the horse, and gently rocked it from side to side. This helped to calm the animal considerably, and in a few seconds the arena was clear.

The gate crew rushed to get into position, and Chris slid up onto his rigging as far as he possibly could. At the same time, he dropped his feet from the rail, being careful not to touch the animal with his spurs, and brought his knees up to a level with the horse's neck. When he was almost ready to call for the gate, his upper leg was parallel with the ground, knees bent ninety degrees, and his feet were resting up at the horse's shoulders, ready to snap out and reach for the "pocket" when the chute was opened.

The chute boss saw he was ready and double checked to make sure the judges were in place and the chute help was watching for the nod.

"Okay, cowboy," he said quietly. "It's your arena."

Chris nodded his head, and the gate slammed open. The horse shied back for just an instant, then, seeing daylight, made its high-dive out into the arena. Chris planted his spurs high into the pocket of the horse's neck for a solid mark, then lay back for a sound spur-ride. He quickly found it would be no ordinary jump-kick ride: this horse bucked like it had eaten gunpowder and kitchen matches for lunch.

Three Below rose up straight into the air and hunched its back into a half-moon, coming down hard and square. Then it jerked around to the left, kind of crow-hopping, never really settling into a good, solid rhythm, then exploded straight up again.

Chris, meanwhile, was trying to get his spurring started, but couldn't get a feel for what Three Below was going to do next. Consequently, he was slightly out of position when the second explosion struck. As the horse went up, Chris rocked back with his feet up high over the withers. He tried to force his feet down again to get a hold, but the rolling action of the beast was too much for him to work against. Then, as the horse reached the top of the jump, Chris's feet fired back down again, rolling him forward ... too far forward, in fact, and when the horse's front feet struck the earth, the jarring concussion threw him over the front end of the brute like a rag-doll. His hand was ripped from the rigging, and he slammed into the arena flat on his face and belly.

Three Below vaulted back into the air, oblivous to the fate of its rider, and came down with one hoof squarely in the middle of Chris's back. As the full weight of the beast came to bear, Chris felt his sternum snap. The horse stumbled slightly and bounded across the arena away from the injured rider.

Instinctively, Chris raised his head and looked around the arena for the horse. Realizing he was safe, he tried to get to his feet. One of the judges ran to him and helped to get him up.

"You okay, cowboy?" he asked, placing Chris's arm over his shoulder.

Chris tried to answer but could not, since the wind had been forced out of his lungs.

"He'll be just fine, ladies and gentlemen," Chris heard the announcer say over the public address system. "Let's have a nice round of applause for Chris. These cowboys certainly are a tough breed, aren't they? Now down in chute four...."

Chris was working to suck a little air back into his lungs when they got him settled against the fence back behind the chutes. He smiled a "thanks" to the cowboys who had helped him out, then gingerly began to assess the injury. He could tell from the pain caused by taking just a small breath that it was going to be serious.

"Chris, are you all right?"

Chris looked up into the face of Royce Smith, a veteran cowboy whom he had admired for years.

"Oh, I guess so," he replied weakly, although he wasn't entirely convinced of that himself. Royce placed a hand on his shoulder and reassured him he would be all right.

Later, Chris's college friends helped him back to the truck, where he crawled into the camper. He tried everything to get comfortable, but to no avail. He was just plain miserable the whole way to Sacramento. He kept wondering if maybe this was God's way of punishing him for his behavior the night before. It never occurred to him that everyone else had been just as bad, if not worse, and *they* weren't hurt!

In Sacramento Chris went to see a doctor, who confirmed that Chris had separated his sternum and gave him some pain pills. It wasn't nearly enough.

Chris took a few of the pills and mounted his first horse. After about two jumps, he could feel his sternum rip loose again, and it was all he could do to hold on until the whistle. He did get a score, but it was well out of the money.

The next night he was determined to do better, so he took six pills and taped his chest together. It worked somewhat, and he managed to finish second for the go-around, qualifying him for the short-go on Sunday. He never wanted anything as badly as this National College title, and he resolved to give that last ride everything he possibly could.

On Sunday, Chris drew a top horse named Headlight, who was a definite money-maker if he could just get by him. He took six more pills and repeated the tape job on his chest from the day before. Then he lowered himself down onto the animal and nodded his head. Headlight was a much more powerful horse than the one from the day before, and all of Chris's preparations went for nothing, as on the third jump out the sternum snapped. Chris's face was twisted in agony, but he resolved not to quit and just kept right on spurring.

After a few more seconds of punishment, his body simply would not tolerate any more, and, nearly unconscious, Chris reached up with is free hand and stopped the ride before the whistle. He eased onto the pick-up horse and staggered back behind the chutes, barely able to breathe.

He had never come so close to winning a big title before, just to watch it slip away simply because his body would not do what he asked of it. Chris needed to sit down, and, feeling as bad as he did, he wanted no company, so he went out behind the bathroom and sat in the grass to try to sort out the details of what had happened. He wondered if he could have done anything different, but the inescapable conclusion was always: he had lost. It was over and done, and nothing he could do now would change that.

He felt the wind brush a tear from his cheek, and he blinked. He hadn't even realized he was crying, but once it was out of his system, he felt refreshed and renewed. No one can hold deep emotions inside for very long without becoming bitter or driven, and a good cry once in a while is just the right medicine for a mental hurt. Chris resolved this would be the last College Finals he would ever lose.

"Just wait till next year," he promised himself. Then, looking up at the sky, he added, "And I promise You I won't be chasin' no women the night before a rodeo, either." He still figured God might be mad at him, and there just wasn't any sense in taking chances.

Chapter 7

Just Riding Through

*Pack up your old guitar, cowboy. Roll up your old sleepin'
      bag.*
It's time you got to movin', 'cause your life is startin' to drag.
*You ain't leavin' nothin' but faces, the same stars watch you
      at night.*
*That same old lonesome will own you, but you've grown too
      tired to fight.*

Pull on your old blue jeans, cowboy, put on your old dusty hat,
Sun-up caught you a-sleepin', gamblin' busted you flat.
*The whiskey, it caught you a-drinkin', the rain and the wind
      caught you cold,*
*Lovin' cost you a memory, and the Devil—he caught your
      soul.*

You're one child's father, another man's son,
One woman's candle of light.
Too far into tomorrow for lovin' somebody tonight.
You're too many miles from home now,
Gamblin' with nothin' to lose.
A side street hobo in rodeo clothes.
Cowboy, you're just riding through.

> Don Cusic (Blackwood Music),
> from **He Rides the Wild Horses**

During the summer of 1968, Chris did very little rodeoing,
partly due to a shortage of ready cash, but mostly due to his

split sternum. After the injury had healed sufficiently, he got a job stacking hay and managed to work for most of the summer. He caught a few scattered rodeos here and there but won less than three hundred dollars all summer.

In the fall, he decided to take a scholarship which had been offered to him by Pat Hamilton, the rodeo sponsor at Sheridan College. He was still having differences with Dale Stiles at Casper, and the scholarship at Sheridan seemed like just the ticket out for Chris.

He soon found himself in another dormitory, this time sharing a room with Bill Larsen. Bill was a rancher's son from Alzada, Montana, who had come up the hard way, losing his father when he was just a boy. He told Chris of how he and his mother, brother and sister had taken over the ranch and made a go of it. Along the way Bill had learned to rope and to ride bucking horses, so he and Chris quickly became the very best of friends.

As the rodeo season got underway that fall, Chris noticed for the first time that he was beginning to really understand what he was doing riding bareback horses—and what he needed to do to get better. He had always had a free-wheeling style of spurring that many referred to as "floppin' and poppin'," with no definitive drag or spur-lick. At some of the summer rodeos, however, Chris had paid close attention to the likes of Clyde Vamvoras and other top hands, noticing that they all made an effort to drag their spurs up the neck, firmly and deliberately, then drive them back down again when they came out at the top. The more he thought about it, the more he realized how much more stability a rider would have with this technique, as well as control provided by the longer contact with the horse's neck during the drag. He began to work hard toward gaining this control and style.

Chris also implemented his first training regimen, complete with diet and exercises, and including a few rather eccentric ideas. He tried drinking a cup of super-strong brewed tea before riding, figuring the concentrated caffeine would provide some sort of boost. For a time he also carried a big jar of honey, from which he would gulp several swallows at the last minute, hoping for a sudden burst of energy. He quit carrying the honey after the jar came open in his gear bag, and he had the sticky goo all over his chaps and spurs.

By the end of the short season, everything was beginning to fall into place, and Chris was starting to feel more comfortable with his new style of riding. Of course, there was a lot more than just rodeo to occupy his time.

Sheridan's social life was a lot more active for Chris than Casper's had been. Maybe it had something to do with the fact that he was no longer a freshman, but he truly enjoyed the feeling of camaraderie that was prevalent at Sheridan. There were still occasional house parties, although they were somewhat subdued compared to the big party at Casper the year before. There was a good deal more casual contact with friends: going to the movies, playing cards, going out for a hamburger and so forth. Chris also developed a keener interest in girls; for the first time since he was a boy, he fell in love.

The young lady's name was Betty Johnson. She was more of a hippie-type than a country girl, but she really liked Chris, and he liked her, so they each tolerated the other's differences. Chris and Betty began dating steadily in mid-October, and for a month they had some pretty good times. Of course, Chris was at school and not out on the road, which always takes its toll on a relationship. But all of that was to change at Thanksgiving time.

Chris and a bulldogger named Joe Rosenburg decided they were going to enter an RCA rodeo in Chicago. Chris scrimped and saved and came up with enough money for his fees in the barebacks and a one-way plane ticket, with a few dollars to spare. Rodeo sponsor Pat Hamilton put up fees for Chris to enter the saddlebronc riding. Joe, too, came up with just enough money for his fees and a dead-end ticket to Chicago. They both agreed that, should either of them win, he would take care of getting the other one back to Sheridan, but if they both lost, they would each be on their own to get a ride home.

They arrived at Chicago's O'Hare International Airport and quickly bought a map of the city. Then they stretched it out in the middle of the terminal floor and tried to figure out where they were going. The biggest problem was the cloudy day: the two country boys couldn't get a bearing from the sun. Consequently, they had no idea in which direction to go from the airport. In despair, they finally asked a local, who put them onto the right bus with instructions on where to get off.

The rodeo grounds were located downtown, near the stockyards, and when Chris and Joe arrived, it was so early the building was not yet unlocked. It was just a little after one in the afternoon, and the rodeo didn't start until seven o'clock that night. They walked across the street to an old run-down bar and grill, which smelled dank and musty and had cob webs hanging from the ceiling.

"Cheery little place," Chris remarked sarcastically.

"Maybe we should wait for the m'aitre d' to seat us," Joe suggested dryly as Chris slid into a booth. They both chuckled and ordered a couple of cheeseburgers and a side of fries, washing it all down with a soft drink.

"Hey, this here's our Thanksgiving dinner," Chris observed, noticing an old T.V. in the corner which was tuned to a football game, reminding him of the date.

"Well, I'll be," said Joe, pausing to examine his cheeseburger for a second before he lopped off another bite. "Happy Thanksgiving, partner."

When they had eaten, they strolled casually back over to the rodeo grounds to wait. After a while, an old hand showed up who was familiar with the Chicago rodeo, and he directed the boys to a nice motel on the lake where everyone would be hanging out. They caught a cab to the motel and within the hour had made friends with a group of cowboys who had rooms there.

"Well, shoot," one of the cowboys said to Chris and Joe, "there ain't no sense you boys taking a room of your own—we got plenty of floor space in our room."

"Well, that'd be just great," Chris replied, gratefully accepting the offer. As it turned out later, there really wasn't "plenty" of room, as there were a total of seven cowboys sharing the room, but somehow they all managed to get by. At present, though, sleeping quarters were the last thing on anyone's mind. In a few hours, they were all down at the rodeo grounds.

The first go-around proved to be quite a disappointment for Chris, as neither he nor Joe placed in the money. Short on cash, they decided they had better come up with a plan—fast.

"Ya know," started Chris thoughtfully, "Dennis Reiners told me I ought to give up riding bucking horses and just pick that old guitar of mine."

"Oh yeah?" answered Joe with a look of surprise. "When did he say that?"

"Oh, back at Sacramento last June," responded Chris, "but I was just thinkin' that mebbe I can pick up a few dollars singing."

"How you gonna get a singing job on this short a notice?"

"Look," began Chris, bending over slightly to keep his voice lower, "we'll get some of the guys together and go into the bar here at the motel, see ...." Chris looked around to see if anyone was listening. "Then I'll start playing m' guitar, with m' hat turned up on a table. You and the boys come up and request a song or two and put a couple of bucks into the hat—seed money. When folks see what we're doing, they'll start putting money in, too."

"Why not?" Joe mused. "Just so long as we get *our* money back."

Chris just laughed. Soon they had a handful of cowboys together, and they went into the bar to try their ploy.

Chicago, it seems, wasn't very receptive to starving cowboys; Chris and his friends didn't make a single dime. They had a pretty good time, though, so the idea hadn't been a total waste.

"Well, I guess Dennis Reiners was dead wrong about my pickin'," Chris said as they left the bar.

"Hey, speaking of Dennis," piped in a voice from behind Chris, "today's his birthday. And I hear they got him a cake over to the rodeo grounds."

Chris could feel the hunger pangs creeping up inside his belly. The thought of a big piece of chocolate cake was overwhelming.

"What're we waiting for?" he responded, picking up the pace.

By the time they got to the rodeo grounds, the last morsel of cake was just being devoured by a hungry cowboy. Chris and his friends watched in despair, until they noticed a couple of cowboys out by the back door who were laughing hysterically. Chris wandered over in their general direction to try and figure out what the joke was all about. Finally he asked one of them, "What's so doggone funny?"

One cowboy caught his breath and looked at Chris. "You eat any of the cake?"

"Well, no . . . but what's that go to do with it?" replied Chris.

"Everything," came the response, as the cowboy broke into hysterics again. "The top layer was made out of Ex-Lax."

Chris looked around. Sure enough, the crowd was thinning quickly, and there was a line outside the bathroom door. For once he was relieved to have been late. He went back to where his friends were standing and shared the news with them. Soon the whole group was doubled over in laughter.

The next day, Chris again placed out of the money and failed to qualify for the short go. He was finished in Chicago, and with $3.50 left to his name, he was beginning to envision himself selling newspapers on a street corner to get up the money for a bus ticket. Joe Rosenburg didn't fare any better, so they parted company after the performance as agreed.

Chris got lucky and caught a ride back to Cheyenne with Jim Steen and John Quintanna, who would be passing through Wyoming on their way back to the Northwest. Chris ate a lot of soup and tightened his belt, making the $3.50 go as far as possible, until he finally arrived in Cheyenne.

In Cheyenne he called a friend and borrowed five dollars for a bus ticket and soon was on his way to Sheridan and home. At the bus depot, he dialed Betty's number; he was going to ask her to come down and pick him up. Her roommate answered the call and informed Chris that Betty was out on a date with someone else. It took Chris nearly two weeks to get over his first broken heart.

A month after Chicago, Chris flew out to Tennessee to visit with Bonnie and Al. It had been about a year since he had seen his parents, and as they were paying for the ticket, Chris decided it was about time he went.

Chris spent hours sharing his rodeo stories with his parents and telling them how his schoolwork was going. By the time he had them completely up to date, they were into the wee hours of the morning.

The next night Al treated everyone to a trip to the Grand Ole Opry at the Rymon Auditorium. Chris heard Waylon Jennings sing "Love of the Common People" and several other top songs, and he heard the old master Marty Robbins perform, as well as many of the Opry regulars. Chris was thrilled by the entire spectacle.

The next day, as there wasn't much to do, Chris pulled out his guitar and began playing a few tunes. Al happened by and paused to listen for a while.

"You know, Chris," Al interrupted after a bit, "you ought to take that old guitar down on Music Row, like all of these other fellows, and see if you can't go talk to some of those record people."

Chris thought about if for a few minutes, then decided to give it a try. He borrowed the car and drove down to Nashville, not exactly sure what he would do once he got there but excited by the prospect of doing anything at all with his music.

Once he parked the car, he roamed up and down Music Row for a while with his guitar. He talked to some of the locals, one of whom told him that what he needed to do was to see a music publisher and get him to listen to his songs. So Chris set out to find a publishing company.

"Well, this looks like as good a prospect as any," he said to himself as he read the sign above the door of one publishing house.

Inside, a pretty young receptionist sat behind a desk. Chris asked her if there would be anyone in who might like to listen to his songs. She smiled up at him and told him to have a seat while she went to find out. A few minutes later she returned and led him into an office in the back. An older, heavyset gentleman stood up behind his desk and shoved out his hand to Chris.

"Come in, young man," he said. "You know, this is quite irregular."

Chris looked at him, somewhat puzzled. "What do you mean?"

"Well," the older man explained, "normally young artists present us with tapes of their music, and we listen to them at our convenience. But since I'm not real busy today, you just go right ahead and play," he finished, motioning for Chris to pick up his guitar and begin.

After hearing three or four songs, the gentleman walked around the desk, and placed a kindly arm around Chris's shoulder. "I'll tell you, son," he began, sounding fatherly, "that 'Bareback Jack' song is pretty well written, but you just don't have much of a market for that type of thing. No, you need to get away from the rodeo stuff and concentrate on commercial sounds." Chris listened attentively to the publisher's every word. "Now, Country music has a certain, repetitive quality . . . you know, it repeats the same line a lot, so folks can sing right along with it if they want. You try writing a few songs like that and give me a call when you have it down pat.''

In a few minutes Chris found himself back out on the street again, shaking his head. He decided the man must certainly know what he was talking about, so he drove back out to the house and sat down to write a commercial song:

She's got a foot like a fist and a hand like a club,
And it hurts when it bounces off of me.
It sure makes me sad when my baby gets mad,
And puts her hand, like a club, onto me.

Chris stared at the words for a few minutes, then crumpled the piece of paper and tossed it into the trash can.

"Shoot, I'll just stick to these old rodeo songs," he decided.

In the spring Chris did fairly well on the college circuit and ended up in second place in the region. This standing qualified him for the National College Finals Rodeo, to be held that year in Deadwood, South Dakota.

Remembering the promise he had made to the Lord the previous year, Chris went directly to the rodeo grounds and didn't stop off to party or chase women on his way to Deadwood. His prudence seemed to pay off, as he placed well in the first two go-arounds and was leading the average going into the short round on Sunday.

LeDoux was only two points ahead of J.C. Trujillo, last year's winner and the reigning champion, which meant that if J.C. could win the round by three points, he would be awarded the title again. If he only won the round by one point over Chris, then J.C. would finish second in the average, and Chris would be the new champion.

J.C. drew a top horse for the short go, and Chris paced nervously behind the chutes while the champion made ready to ride. Finally, he nodded his head, and the gate swung open. The bronc twisted and kicked, but J.C. stayed right with him through the first few jumps. Then he began to slip, just slightly, off to one side. As the whistle blew, he was pretty far off to the side but had maintained a good spur-lick throughout the ride. The judges awarded him sixty-three points for his effort.

The rest of the competition was fading fast, as low scores and goose-eggs dwindled the ranks of the other finalists. When Chris finally lowered himself down into the chute, he knew a score of sixty-two or better would clinch the title for him. He remember the promise he had made to himself the year before out behind the bathroom—to win the title this year.

He slid up onto the rigging and nodded his head. The horse was not a spectacular draw and just jump-kicked out across the arena, but Chris put all his heart into spurring the animal. After the ride, he looked expectantly towards the announcer's booth, waiting for his score.

"Ladies and gentlemen," came the hoped-for announcement, "the judges have awarded Chris sixty-two points for that ride; let's have a nice round of applause for our new National Collegiate Bareback Riding Champion!"

Chris couldn't believe it—he had done it! His face exploded into an ear-to-ear grin. Then he paused for just a second and glanced towards the heavens in a moment of silent thanks.

Later that summer Chris entered the big Cheyenne Frontier Days Rodeo. For him, Cheyenne would always be something special, and this year in particular was to be a special treat.

In the first go-around, Chris had drawn a horse named Chicken-Fry, a spicy old cayuse that put on as good a show in the chutes as it did in the arena. As Chris tightened up his spurs and chaps, he watched the horse snorting and stomping around in the chute. It was the sort of intimidating behavior an old veteran horse could use to take the will out of a younger, less experienced rider. Chris knew it was just an act. There were very few horses that gave an honest indication of what they would do in the arena by how they behaved in the chutes. Sometimes the most vicious chute fighters just scattered and ran in the arena, and the most gentle, well-mannered chute horses would nearly rip their riders' arms off when the gate was cracked open.

Chris rosined up his glove and climbed onto the chute to pat a small amount of the powdery substance on the rigging handle. He looked down the line and saw there were still a few minutes to wait, as they were just opening the gate three chutes up from his position.

LeDoux reached down into the chute, grabbed a handful of mane, and watched the rider out in the arena. He began patting his horse on the neck with his other hand to get the animal settled down before he mounted it.

Every cowboy will tell you the most dangerous time to be on roughstock is in the chutes. If they act up and a cowboy goes down, there is no place to get away from the bronc's or bull's crushing hooves. For this reason, it is very important to be as careful as possible while getting ready for the ride. As the chute boss moved up to the chute ahead of him, Chris lowered himself down onto his horse and slipped his glove on. He tied off the glove thong just as the gate of the chute before his clanged open, spilling its explosive contents out into the arena.

Chris ran his hand up into the handle, using his free hand to help pull his fingertips through the snug opening. Taking a firm grip, he rolled his wrist toward himself, locking the hand in place.

He looked up just in time to see the rider being swept to the ground by the pick-up man. He could sense the flank man behind him adjusting the flank strap as the horse perked up its ears and stamped its feet in protest. Then the chute help swarmed around the gate, making ready for the irrevocable nod of the head from the rider within.

Chris slid up onto his rigging as far as he could, squeezing along the horse's withers with his knees, his feet hanging down toward the bronc's shoulders. With his free hand he made an almost unconscious adjustment to his hat, then looked out into the arena to make sure everything was set. The chute boss caught his eye, and the big man signaled that the arena was clear. Chris focused his attention on a spot on the bronc's neck just in front of the withers, and nodded his head.

The gate latch slammed free and the gate was pulled open. The horse hesitated just a split second, then blew into the arena. Chris locked his spurs into the animal's neck for two full jumps, then lay back and went to spurring.

Chicken-Fry had a smooth action, and Chris was able to open up for the judges with his wild style of spurring. After the whistle, he pulled himself upright with his free hand and slipped off onto the pick-up horse. He was awarded sixty-eight points for the ride and ended up in third place for the go-around.

The next day, out by the secretary's office, Chris was looking at the draw sheets to find out what he had drawn for the next performance.

"What'd you get today, Chris?" asked a voice from behind him.

Chris turned around to see Paul Mayo, one of his long-time cowboy heroes, and couldn't believe Paul actually knew his name. In the few short years that Chris had been going to the RCA rodeos, he really hadn't fallen in with any groups or made a lot of friends; he just went to the rodeos, rode and went home, for the most part. He never realized anyone had noticed him, and particularly not a World Champion like Paul Mayo. Chris was thrilled.

Chris finished out of the money in the rest of the go-arounds at Cheyenne that year, but being recognized by Paul Mayo and some of the other top cowboys had made the whole rodeo a memorable experience.

Chapter 8

Real Live Buckeroo

Well, I ain't the type of cowboy that you'll see on T.V.,
I wasn't near as pretty as Mama wanted me to be.
Well, I grew up on the ranches, just cussin' all day long,
Breakin' in them broomtails and hummin' old dirty songs,
Whiskey tends to make me high, and sad songs make me cry,
And pretty women break my heart almost every night.
Yeah, I run on beans and nicotine, I'm a real live buckeroo,
And my heart's not pure and my boots ain't clean
And I never tell the truth.

Well, if there's anything under my hat besides the cattle biz,
Well, I just can't seem to remember what it is.
Yeah, my thinkin's kinda crude, but my lovin' gets plumb
  rank,
Them girlies just don't understand me a-snortin' 'round their
  flanks.
And when I take a nasty fall, I'll cuss until I'm blue,
Then I'll get right up and on again, just like you're s'posed
  to do.
But it ain't because I'm so brave—all that stuff's just talk,
My daddy says the reason is,
I'm dumber than a box of rocks.

Gary McMahan (Yodeling Yahoo Music)
from **Songs of Rodeo & Country**

At the college finals in Deadwood, Chris met Willie Britton, the rodeo coach of Eastern New Mexico State University in Portales. Since Sheridan was only a two-year college, Chris knew he would have to be moving along in the fall of 1969, but he really hated to let go of the friends he had made in Wyoming. However, since E.N.M.U. offered him a full rodeo scholarship, he accepted the proposition.

Another factor that influenced Chris's decision was that E.N.M.U. was primarily an art school. Chris had always loved drawing and sculpting, so he figured this might be a great way to learn more about these subjects while pursuing his primary avocation—rodeo.

Chris moved down to New Mexico, after a pretty successful summer of rodeoing, with over twelve hundred dollars in his pockets. His new roommate was Matt Mills, who was from Pampa, Texas. Although a roper, Matt had ridden a few bareback horses, and he and Chris soon became good friends.

The schoolwork at Eastern New Mexico was much more strenuous than Chris was accustomed to, and he really had to work hard to keep his grades up. Maybe working harder made him decide to play a bit harder, but he finally cut loose from his tee-totaling ways and began to carouse a bit more than usual.

One night, Matt and Chris went to a party with Jim Parker, Marvin Schulte and Butch Cody, along with several other people. The house was a traditional adobe, complete with strings of peppers hanging from the porch rafters to dry in the warm breeze.

As the party got into full swing, Chris, art major that he was, decided to show off his technique by drawing a few bareback horses—on the walls of the house. Someone else decided to see just how thick the adobe was and began punching holes in the interior walls.

The house had just been rented for the semester, so there was little furniture to speak of. As the alcohol began to assert itself, the cowboys' stories about rodeo and ranch life got meaner and wilder. Then challenges were thrown down about who was better than whom, and so on. To end the argument, one of the ropers' horses was brought into the living room and rigged up with a bareback rigging. Everyone took turns on the horse, pretending to spur it out across the living room. Needless to say, it was turning into a pretty wild night.

Portales is located in a dry county, so any liquor to be found there has to be brought down from nearby Clovis or purchased at a premium rate from local bootleggers. As it turned out, the booze ran short at this particular party, and since most of the women had already left when the horse had been brought into the room, Chris came up with a unique idea to solve the problem of what to do next.

"Okay everybody," he stammered loudly. "Here's what we're gonna do." He looked around to make sure he had everyone's attention. "We got just one bottle of whiskey left, so we're gonna have us a little contest to see who's the biggest, baddest cowboy in town. Winner gets the bottle."

Everyone's curiosity was piqued, so they gathered around to hear the proposed contest. "Everyone get out your tobacco, take a plug, and pass it on to the next guy. Everybody takes a bit of everybody else's snuff or chewing tobacco, until we all got a big mouthful. Then, whenever you spit, you lose. The last guy to spit gets the whiskey."

All present cheered their consent and started passing around the bags, pouches and cans. They had Copenhagen, Skoal, Day's Work, Beechnut, and Brown Mule, just to name a few. Right away, the contestants began dropping out, as the mixture proved too noxious for many of the young cowboys to handle.

Finally, there remained only two contestants still seated at the trash can brought in for the losers: Chris and another big cowboy named Buck. They stared across the trash can at each other with alcohol-hazed eyes like a pair of bullfrogs, each ready to burst. Suddenly, Buck let go and choked his load into the trash can—immediately followed by Chris. They stared back up at each other, grateful the ordeal was ended, and Chris picked up his bottle of whiskey. But by this time, he was far too sick to appreciate the liquor; he gave his prize away and skulked off into the darkness of the night to find a place to curl up and die.

In the morning, Chris swore he'd never get that drunk again, but come Friday night there'd be another party, and again he'd end up right in the thick of it. The parties were not always as wild as the "big party," but there was always some roping and arm-wrestling, and plenty of serious drinking.

As September waned, Chris noticed he was putting on a few extra pounds around the middle and decided to do something about it. During a rabbit-hunting expedition with a local named Mike Gordon, he came upon the perfect idea for losing weight.

"Hey Mike," he said. "I've got a proposition to make you."

"Yeah, what's that?" responded Mike, turning to Chris curiously.

"Let's make a bet to see if we can live off of the land for a full week," Chris explained. "You know, not eat anything that we don't pick, kill or catch ourselves."

Looking at the two rabbits they had already killed, Mike agreed to the wager.

That weekend they ate well, and on Sunday night they headed back toward Portales.

As the truck reached the outskirts of town, Mike suddenly slammed on the brakes, nearly throwing Chris through the windshield.

"What the heck?" snapped Chris, bracing himself as the truck powered into a U-turn.

"You hungry?" Mike asked, a sly smile playing across his face.

"Yeah, but what are you doing?" Chris answered. As the truck slowed, the headlights came to rest on a large rattlesnake coiled up on the edge of the warm tarmac. Mike grabbed his .22 rifle from the window rack and stepped out of the truck. The soft crack of the rifle faded in to the starlit sky, and Mike came trotting back to the truck with the dead snake dragging behind.

"Let's go cook this son-of-a-gun," he said. He tossed the reptile into the bed of the truck, and they pointed the vehicle back toward town.

In a few miles they came to the outskirts of a modern housing development situated on the edge of Portales. A few hundred feet away was an old, torn-down farmhouse, reduced to its foundation and a few feet of crumbled walls on three sides. It would provide an adequate windbreak for a fire. The boys pulled off the road and soon had a blaze going in the ruins.

Mike cleaned the snake and coiled it around a stick for roasting over the open fire, while Chris scavenged up enough wood to make certain the fire stayed plenty hot for the time necessary to cook the creature.

As the meat popped and sizzled over the open flame, Chris and Mike began to tell old rodeo stories. Suddenly, they heard a bit of commotion behind them, and a boy on a bicycle came riding up to check out the fire.

"Whatcha guys doin'?" he asked cautiously from the edge of the house, ready to ride off at the slightest hint of provocation.

"Cookin' us up some dinner, partner," replied Chris.

"Yeah? Whatcha got there?" asked the youngster.

"Rattlesnake," answered Mike seriously.

"Naw, you ain't got no rattlesnake," he said doubtfully. Chris reached down for the skin and rattles and tossed them toward the boy.

"Take a look for yourself, friend," Chris said.

Curiosity got the better of the boy, and he decided the two cowboys were safe enough, so he set down his bicycle and bent over to more closely examine the snakeskin.

"Well, I'll be . . .," he said, walking carefully over to the campfire. There he saw the body wrapped around the stick, snapping and popping over the fire. Suddenly he darted toward his bicycle. "Ain't nobody gonna believe this! You guys wait right here."

Chris and Mike just laughed and turned back to their fire. Shortly, the boy returned with several of his friends. They approached cautiously . . . all except the one who had been there previously. He just marched right into camp as if he owned the place and nodded to Chris and Mike.

"Like you to meet some of m' friends," he said, turning towards his companions. "C'mon already, I told you the snake is dead and bein' cooked. He sure as heck ain't gonna bite you now."

The others moved in a little closer, examined the skin and rattles, and looked at the meat cooking over the fire.

"Are you really gonna eat that?" one of them asked.

"Well sure they are," answered the leader of the group, then turning towards Chris he finished, "aren't you boys?"

"You bet," answered Mike. "Nothing' like rattler to fill a body up."

"Say, just where you fellers from, anyway?" asked the boy with the bike.

Chris's eyes began to twinkle as he felt a good story coming on. He turned to Mike and winked. "Why don't you finish cookin' supper while I tell our company about Daddy, and the ranch."

Mike grinned and nodded his approval.

"You see, boys," Chris turned to face his audience and motioned with his hands for them all to gather in a little closer to the fire. "Me and m' brother Mike have spent our whole lives up on a ranch, 'way out in the desert. Why, we've never even been to town before, not in our whole entire lives."

"Aw, c'mon mister," one disbelieving voice came from the crowd. "Then where'd you get the truck?" A few others piped in their approval of the question.

"Well ya see, Daddy kept us up on that ranch all the time, a-raisin' horses and cattle, and one day a feller come out in this truck wantin' to buy some horses. Well, Daddy said we didn't have no use for no money, since we never went to town anyways, but he'd trade him a dozen horses for this here pickup truck.''

The boys all nodded their heads, satisfied with the answer, so Chris continued, "Of course, none of us knew how to drive it, and Daddy swore he'd tan us both good if'n we ever tried to learn—he was afraid we'd go to town, ya know—but when he'd be off in the high country chasin' strays, why, we played around with it some and finally figured out how to make it go.''

Catching a few doubting looks from the gallery, Chris added, "Why, it's really easy. I s'pose you boys all know how to do it?'' Now, what ten-year-old boy would admit that he didn't know how to drive? Whatever doubt they had about Chris's story melted away.

"So what're you doin' here tonight?'' someone asked.

"Well, a few years ago Daddy died, but he told us that when he died he'd still be a-watchin' over us, to make sure we didn't fight and didn't go to town or nothin'. There was many a night his old ghost would come back a wanderin' around the place, just makin' sure that me and Mike had done our chores. Why, we was plumb scared out of our wits most of the time, wasn't we, Mike?''

"Boy, I tell ya, we slept in the same bedroom 'cause neither one of us was brave enough to go off and sleep alone,'' Mike added with a sly smile.

The boys in the group all nodded their agreement that they, too, would have slept in the same room if there was a ghost running loose on the place.

"Well anyway,'' the storyteller continued, "last night was the worse yet. Mike forgot to feed the chickens . . . .''

"Hey, wait a minute, you said you was gonna do it,'' Mike interrupted.

"All right,'' Chris conceded, "one of us forgot to feed the chickens, and Daddy just got madder than heck. He was throwing things around and slamming doors. Why, we were just terrified, so we ran out, jumped into the truck and took off—running for our very lives, I think.''

They all nodded that it had definitely been time to get out of there.

"Well, we been a-drivin' all day, and now we finally got here," Chris said, stretching out his arms with his palms turned up toward the sky, ". . . town."

The boys all looked at each other.

"Yeah, we've always wondered what town would be like," Chris continued as he walked around the old ruin, looking at the walls and gazing off at the lights of the housing development. "Yup, it's everything we imagined, ain't it, little brother?"

"Boy, it's really something, all right," agreed Mike, taking the snake from the fire. "Why, I just . . . well, I'm just beside myself."

"Oh no," voiced one of the boys, waving his hands in front of his face. "This ain't town. Town is way over there. This ain't nothing out here, just an old burned-out house, is all."

Chris and Mike looked at each other open-mouthed. Both gasped in unison, "You're kidding?"

"No, really," the boy continued, eager now to help these poor dumb country boys get out into the real "town." "You gotta keep driving up this road for a few miles until you come to a stoplight. You know what a stoplight is?"

Mike handed Chris a big chunk of meat. They both stared at the spokesman with blank looks on their faces, indicating they didn't know.

"Well," the boy went on to explain, using his hands as a guide, "it's about this big, and it hangs down in the middle of the road, where it crosses another road. It's got three different colored lights on it: red, yellow and green, but only one light comes on at a time. Now, if the light is green, well, you just go right on through, but if it's red, you gotta stop and wait for it to turn green, or else you'll go to jail."

Mike and Chris studied the boy's face very intently as they ate their meal, absorbing every word.

"What's jail?" asked Chris.

"Trust me, it's a bad place," said the boy, realizing this would be too big a job even for him to handle, "and you don't want to go there. If the light is red, you stop until it turns green, got it?"

Chris and Mike nodded that they understood.

"Good," finished the boy. "Well, when you get to the light, you'll be in town."

Then, hearing a faraway voice, one of the boys jumped up and announced he had to go home. The others all agreed it was time for them to be going as well. Chris and Mike shook hands with each and every one of them and bade them farewell.

After the last boy was out of earshot, Chris and Mike let loose the laughter that had been building up since the story began. They then finished their meal and headed home.

The snake was to be the last meal they had for the next three days, since there was hardly an abundance of wild game on the campus. Finally, Chris called Mike and asked him if he was hungry.

"You're darn right, I am," Mike retorted testily.

"What do you say we go for a pizza?" said Chris, tacitly offering to drop the bet.

"I'll meet you there in ten minutes," came the reply.

The boys ate pizza, pecan pie and ice cream until they were fairly bursting. But Chris had managed to shed a few pounds during the week, so the bet hadn't been a total waste.

As the reigning National Collegiate Bareback Champion, Chris did a terrific job of living up to the title: he managed to finish up in the money in nearly every college rodeo that fall, in both the barebacks and the saddlebroncs, and he really had a good time in the Southwest.

He also got in a few RCA rodeos, such as the time he and Matt Mills drove up to Guymon, Oklahoma. It was during this drive Chris penciled the words to "Them Bareback Horses," although the music didn't come along until later.

Soon, however, the short fall season was over, and it was back to schoolwork again for Chris and the other members of the team. After about a month without rodeos, several of them got together and decided it was time to head out. They figured they should get a taste of the tropics, if they were going to take off rodeoing, so they entered a rodeo in Miami, Florida.

Chris, Marvin Schulte and Butch Cody left Portales in Sid Savage's pickup truck, with a homemade camper shell on back and Sid driving. After packing in all of their gear, two riders could fit comfortably in the back on a mattress, and the other two rode up front.

As they headed down the road across Texas, Louisiana and Mississippi, visions of palm trees and beautiful young women in bikinis raced through their minds. They drove through swampy wetlands and watched the sun rise over the Atlantic Ocean, soaking up that warm Florida sunshine and often stopping to pick oranges or coconuts from groves along the way.

Upon reaching the outskirts of Miami, the cowboys pulled off near a beach motel and rented a room, not realizing they had chosen a spot in what was predominently a Cuban retirement community. Eagerly, they scanned the beaches and shopping centers for miles, looking for those bikinis, but all they found were eighty-year-old grandmothers comparing illnesses and injuries. The boys were sorely disappointed.

The rodeo was just more horse manure and gunsmoke, and none of the boys won anything at all. To make matters worse, Sid broke his collarbone and had to be taken to the hospital for treatment.

By the time they finally left the hospital, the four New Mexico transplants were ready to hit the trail. Sid crawled into the back of the truck and the others squeezed into the cab, taking turns with the driving. Chris could appreciate Sid's pain, remembering his own torturous truckride to Sacramento a few years ago when he had split his sternum.

Pulling into Portales a few days later, Chris thought about how good it always felt to get back home again after a rodeo;

home was simply a place where your meals were already paid
for. On the other hand, Chris wasn't really looking forward
to going back to his classes. Rodeo was beginning to take over
his life, and he felt if he could just get a good show or two
under his belt, he'd be able to make it as a pro. For the moment, however, he went ahead and registered for the spring
semester.

The next rodeo was a few weeks later in Denver. Chris managed to sneak a ride up and enter the bareback riding; although
he didn't win anything, he had a good ride and was feeling
pretty confident of his abilities. A few weeks later, in January,
he flew over to Ft. Worth for the big rodeo there. He ended
up staying in a two-dollar room at the Liberty Hotel in the
slum section of the city with winos and derelicts for neighbors.
In the morning, he quickly caught a cab to the rodeo grounds
and just hung around all day, waiting for the performance
to start.

It turned out to be well worth the wait, as he won nearly
five hundred dollars, the most he'd ever made at a single time
in a rodeo. Chris caught a bus back to Portales with plenty
of jingle in his pockets and a heavy decision weighing on his
mind. He knew what he wanted to do, but he also knew how
much trouble it would cause with his parents if he told them
he was going to quit school and rodeo full time.

A few days later, he reached his decision and placed that
dreaded collect phone call back to Tennessee. His father
answered, and they shared small talk for a few minutes, but
Al could tell something big was up.

"What's the matter, son?" he asked pointedly.

Chris had been purposefully stalling, knowing his father
would explode when he learned what Chris had in mind. For
years Al had stressed the importance of staying in school, and
now Chris had to break the bad news to him.

"Dad," he began, "I hate to tell you this, but I'm going
to quit school ... I'm gonna start rodeoing professionally."

There was a long silence at the other end, and Chris noticed his palms were sweating profusely.

"Well," Al said finally, "sounds good. Sounds like you have an opportunity to make some money, so go ahead. You can always go back to school in a year or two."

Chris nearly dropped the phone. He couldn't believe his father was actually giving him his blessing—but the young cowboy didn't argue. After hanging up the phone he let out a holler and threw his hat in the air.

"Watch out, America," he said to himself. "Here I come!"

Grandma Gingrich

Grandpa Gingrich

photo courtesy of ProRodeo Hall of Champions

Chris on his second-ever saddle bronc horse at Burns Run, Oklahoma, in 1964.

photo courtesy "The Thunderbird"

1968 THUNDERBIRD COWBOYS: Carrying the Casper College banner into the arena on the spring circuit were these team members (left to right): Charles Winters, Keith Maddox, Gary Hamilton, Chris LeDoux, Jack Eicks, T. J. Walter, Scott Maller and Dave Craig, with veteran coach and regional director Dale Stiles. Part of the potential of the 1968 Rodeo Season is tied up in some other freshmen who compete as individuals: Doug Wilson, Allen Gaddis, Jay Mader and Pat Miller. Real comers!

photo courtesy of ProRodeo Hall of Champions

Chris won first place on this ride at Pueblo, Colorado, riding for
Sheridan College in 1969.

Ferrell Butler; photo courtesy of
ProRodeo Hall of Champions

The 1970 NFR bareback riders (from left to right, starting with the back row): Dale Trotter, Jay Himes, Chris LeDoux, John Edwards, T.J. Walter, Royce Smith, Jim Ivory, Bob Mayo, Jim Dix, Larry Mahan, Joe Alexander, Ace Berry, Clyde Vamvoras, Gary Tucker, Paul Mayo.

Gustafson Rodeo Photography; photo courtesy of
ProRodeo Hall of Champions

Cheyenne Frontier Days always held a special significance to Chris. In 1971 he took this trip aboard Ditch Witch.

Bern Gregory; photo courtesy of ProRodeo Hall of Champions

John "Witch" Holman, Tom Tate and Chris behind the chutes at the 1971 NFR.

Peggy's graduation picture, 1971.

Peggy and Clay, 1972.

Foxie the Rodeo Photographer; photo courtesy of ProRodeo Hall of Champions

Chris and Peggy drove all the way to San Diego on bald tires, arriving nearly broke, for this ride on Southern Pride in 1973. The gamble paid off with eighty-two points, first place, and over eight hundred dollars in prize money.

Al Long; photo courtesy of ProRodeo Hall of Champions

Chris on Reg Kessler's legendary Three Bars at the 1973 NFR. Three Bars won this particular match, though Chris did ride him out at Houston in 1977.

A monument to Chris's patience, the cabin in Kaycee still stands today.

Chris Brandt; photo courtesy of ProRodeo Hall of Champions

Chris and Clay behind the chutes. They became a pretty common sight together.

photo courtesy of ProRodeo Hall of Champions

T.J. Walter turned in one of his better NFR performances on Arapahoe, earning seventy-nine points.

I met Chris LeDoux at a high school rodeo in New Castle, Wyoming. At first I thought he was a little strange; apparently, he had spent the night in a pig barn and had no money. But the one thing I really noticed about him was that he was just a happy-go-lucky kind of guy. And after I saw him ride that day, I knew that he had a whole lot of talent.

We soon became the best of friends. There was nothing that we didn't do together. We lived in Kaycee together and rodeoed all over the world together.

Like many best friends, there were times when I could have killed him—the only thing wrong was that he was too darn big to whip. There were also times when he embarrassed me to death. But in the end, we would always get even with each other, one way or another!

There were many times that I saw Chris ride a bucking son-of-a-gun. Nobody at the rodeos was prouder of him that I was when he would go out and make a great ride.

Many times we would argue over little things, but the biggest arguments would arise when it was time to leave a rodeo. First of all, Chris never wanted to drive, and second, when he did decide to drive, he would scare a man to death! But when we were traveling down the road, if he had ten dollars in his pocket, half of that would belong to me. He would give me anything he had, and I would do the same.

When we were young and rodeoing, we both had set two goals: one was to make the Finals together, and the other was to win the World Championships together. Since we were both in different events, that was pretty easy to agree upon. Well, we both did make the Finals together the first year we went, but somewhere along the line Chris got ahead of me and went on to win the World in the bareback riding. I can remember the year he won; I never made the Finals that year, so he called me on the phone to give me the news. He was the happiest guy in the world!

Now that our lives have faded away from rodeo and we are both out trying to accomplish other goals in our lives, I don't get a chance to see Chris much anymore. But once in a while I'll run into him at Kaycee, and we sit around reminiscing and telling old rodeo stories.

In closing, I would like just to wish Chris the very best of luck with his singing career. I hope that he reaches the highest of goals, as he did in rodeo. One thing I'd like to say about Chris LeDoux was that when they made him, I'm sure that the mold was broke, because I have never met anybody like him. He is definitely one of a kind!

Witch Holman
July 27, 1985

I really enjoyed reading *Gold Buckle Dreams*. It brought back a lot of memories.

There are a lot of things that I though of as I was reading, things that, if they were added to the book, no one would believe!

This particular book is a good accounting of Chris's life as I know it—a young man who started with nothing but a lot of determination and succeeded.

I'm proud of Chris and happy for him. It was a pleasure to have spent a part of my life with him.

T.J. Walter
April 5, 1986

James Fain; photo courtesy of ProRodeo Hall of Champions

Ronnie "Punch" Rossen, then World Champion Bullrider, out on Kerby's bull L.

James Fain; photo courtesy of ProRodeo Hall of Champions

J.C. Trujillo at Pendleton aboard the Christensen Brothers' Smith and Velvet.

Molly Brown, Phoenix, Arizona, 1976: "the horse that pulled my collarbone apart."

Claude Long; photo courtesy of ProRodeo Hall of Champions

Chris won first place in the go-around for this eighty-point ride on Grinning Bird at the 1976 NFR.

Newly crowned World Champion Chris LeDoux just after the tenth go-around of the 1976 NFR, with Lon Keating (left) and J.C. Trujillo. Note J.C.'s broken hand.

James Fain; photo courtesy of ProRodeo Hall of Champions

"It Ain't the Years—It's the Miles"—Chris at Evanston, Wyoming, in 1976.

photo courtesy of American Cowboy Songs

Chris LeDoux, "The Singing Bronc Rider," Salt Lake City, 1978.

Chapter 9

Goin' and a-blowin'

I'm a-goin' and a-blowin' and a-headin' down the road,
Tryin' to make a living rodeoing.
I been a-drivin' all night, 'neath the pale moonlight,
Waitin' for the sun to start showin'.
There's too many miles, and not enough time,
But I'm gonna make it just the same.
It's a mighty tough life, but I like it all right,
You know I wouldn't have it any other way.

Well, I been drinkin' that old black coffee,
Till it tastes like turpentine.
I've heard every song on the Bill Mack Show,
Pert' near fifty times.
And a little green man on a motorcycle,
I passed a little while a go,
Oh, I could sure use some sleep, but I gotta keep
A-headin' on down the road.

It's drive up, get out, and get on another one,
And boy you'd better win,
'Cause your money's gettin' low and the banker gets mad
When them hot checks start rolling in.
Well, ain't life great on this interstate,
Lookin' out for Smokey the Bear.
Flying high on caffeine and Copenhagen,
And breathin' that cool night air.

Chris LeDoux (Wyoming Brand Music)
from **Songbook of the American West**

Chris stared out the bus window, watching the flat Texas prairie near Lubbock and Abilene pass by. It had only been a few days since he left Ft. Worth, returning to Portales, and now he was leaving college life behind him forever to return to Ft. Worth and start his professional rodeo career. He remembered the day he had stood in the empty house in Cheyenne after his mother had left for Tennessee. Freedom felt good—but scary as well.

Chris hadn't really given much thought to what he was going to do now that he was "out on the road"; he only had a few hundred dollars and no car, but he was sure he'd figure something out. John Forbes and Witch Holman had been at the Ft. Worth rodeo and said they would be sticking around a few days before heading on to their next one. Chris figured he'd fall in with them for a day or two until he was really going strong.

In the early seventies, the RCA (now the PRCA) had no system for "buddying-up," so it was difficult for cowboys to travel together. Chris, Witch and John tried to stick together, but they usually would just end up crossing trails at different rodeos for a night or two before going off in different directions again. In the winter of 1970, the rodeos came fast and furious for Chris.

Behind the chutes, first at Ft. Worth and then at San Antonio, Chris gazed in fascination at the names carved on the walls: Clyde Vamvoras, Tex Martin, Jim Shoulders—and hundreds of sets of initials that could belong to just about any one of Chris's rodeo hereos. It was a magic time for Chris, who went to the places he had always read about and competed with the cowboys he had always emulated.

From San Antonio, the three moved on to Houston and the Astrodome. Chris was awed by the "Eighth Wonder of the World," as it was billed then. Houston was a major rodeo which lasted for over a week, so Chris found that there was time to enter a few other rodeos while it was going on. He and his friends set up a base camp of sorts in Houston and popped out to various rodeos between go-arounds.

Chris teamed up with Delane Nixon to hitch a ride first to Jackson, Mississippi, then on to Baton Rouge, Louisiana. Along the way, the boys were immersed in varying cultures and customs which merged one into another as quickly as you'd change clothes. In Louisiana, for example, they experienced "Cajun Coffee," a bitter, chicory-enriched drink to be slowly savored, not gulped. This they found out the hard way, ordering the drink by mistake. But they swallowed it heartily, not wanting to look like fools.

At Baton Rouge, Chris met Ronie "Punch" Rossen, a mighty bull rider and a World Champion. Ronnie agreed to give Chris and another bareback rider named Larry Hodge a lift to Amarillo, as he was going to Denver after the rodeo. Delane managed to catch a ride to Montana, so he and Chris parted company.

That night, as Chris and Larry watched the bull-riding event, they paid particular attention to Ronnie's ride. Punch had drawn a pretty good bull, which fired hard at first, then began to slow up in its attack. He decided it was time to show off his gold-buckle style and began spurring the bull with reckless abandon. The action re-ignited the fire in the animal, and just as the whistle sounded, it exploded into a second fit. Punch, caught slightly out of position, was tossed forward, and as the bull spun back around, his cheek was impaled on one of its horns.

The blow knocked Punch out cold. Blood spurting from his face, he flopped to the ground, jerking around like a stuck pig.

"Oh, hell," Chris remarked, grabbing the fence and pressing his face closer for a better view of the arena. "I think he's dead."

Larry just watched spellbound as the clowns worked the bull away from the stricken rider so the ambulance crew could move in. "Well, there goes our ride to Amarillo," he said, with an attempt at humor to bring them both out of their shock.

"Yeah, I guess we're on our own," Chris said with a forced laugh.

They moved back behind the chutes, where Ronnie had regained consciousness and was getting his wound treated with iodine and soapy water.

"Forget it," they heard him say to the medic. "I ain't goin' to no hospital. It's just a flesh wound. Shoot, I been hurt worse shavin'."

The ambulance driver just shook his head; he'd been through this before with these rodeo cowboys, and he knew that, unless he was out cold, there'd be almost no way to take any hard-riding cowboy to the doctor or hospital. "If you want to ride another bull in the next week, you're gonna have to have some stitches in that cheek to hold it all together. I can't do that here—you're gonna have to come to the hospital and see the doctor ... unless, of course, you'd rather sit out a few rodeos."

"All right, all right," Punch relented. "But I'm just getting a few stitches, then checking out, right?"

The ambulance driver nodded his head, and the patient was prepared for transport.

In addition to the hole in his cheek, Punch had also taken a pretty hard blow to the forehead, just above his eye, where he had hit the bull's skull after being impaled on the short horn. It, too, was bleeding and beginning to swell, and the medics would clean it up on the ride to the emergency room.

No cowboy means to cause grief to these hard-working, conscientious medical people. But cowboys and medics ascribe to conflicting views where injuries are concerned. Medics believe you should stop everything and get immediate medical attention, even for the slightest injury, since there's no way to tell just how serious it might be. They're probably right, but cowboys look at an injury, no matter how serious, as just another part of the sport: an inconvenience that has to be tolerated but shouldn't take up too much of their time. The important thing is to get on down the road to the next rodeo.

Due to these differing philosophies, many an ambulance driver has thrown his hands up in exasperation and gone off cursing a hard-headed cowboy.

As Chris and Larry approached the wounded bull rider, the medic was just helping Punch into the back of the ambulance.

"How're you doing?" asked Chris, with a look of concern.

"Well, I think I'm in the money, but I doubt that I'll win it," remarked Punch with a grin.

"No," said Chris, a bit confused, "I mean your face."

"Something wrong with my face?" Punch asked in mock surprise. Then, beginning to laugh, he slapped Chris on the shoulder. "It's gonna take a lot more than this little scratch to slow me down."

Chris looked at the bandages on his face and remembered the spurting blood in the arena. "Some scratch," he said quietly.

"Say," said Ronnie, changing the subject, "have you boys tried these Lou'siana oysters yet?"

Chris and Larry looked at each other and shook their heads.

"Well, as soon as I get back, we'll go to town and toss a few down." Later, they found out that Ronnie *had* won the bull riding.

The next day, as they drove down the road to Amarillo, Ronnie kept turning the rearview mirror down to look at his face. He had already removed the bandages, figuring the wound would heal faster in the fresh air. But there seemed to be a second reason for removing the dressings.

"Doggone, that sure is a good-looking son-of-a-gun," he remarked, looking at his swollen, battered face in the mirror.

Ronnie dropped the boys off in Amarillo before he headed back out toward Denver. In a few days, Chris and Larry were back in Houston for the final go, then off to another major rodeo in El Paso. From that base, they sallied forth to other rodeos, such as Scottsdale, Arizona, always returning to their main rodeo.

Chris wrote a letter home to his folks during that period, and as he placed a stamp on the envelope, he looked at the corner where the return address should go. After thinking for a few minutes, he drew a small outline of the United States and placed a question mark in the center of it.

In those days, rodeo had no central entry system, as there is today, where all rodeos are entered through a single phone number. Often cowboys would spend up to eight hours a day in a phone booth on the side of the road, trying to get through to a rodeo secretary in some remote little town half a continent away. Each rodeo had to be entered separately, and there was no coordination as to the times the rodeo office would be open. Once entered, there were always mix-ups and confusion, but the rodeo secretaries did the best they could to keep everything under control.

But there were also some advantages to rodeoing in the early seventies, the most notable being the fact that there were considerably fewer contestants. Cowboys became a very tight-knit group, much like a family, and with fewer rodeos to go to, they could often take several days off to spend in one location, such as Denver or Calgary, for a little mischief and carousing. The married men could take along their wives, do some sight-seeing or camping along the way, and still be competitive in the standings by entering only sixty or seventy rodeos per year.

Chris, for all of his efforts, had a pretty rough go of it, financially, during that first winter. He always seemed to win just enough to get him to the next show; of course, that was all that mattered to him at the time. With a cold can of pork-n-beans, his thumb in the air, and fees for the next rodeo in his pocket, he was content. He realized, though, that he would have to start winning consistently if he wanted to become competitive in a serious way—and to do that, he was going to have to change his riding style. The problem was, he just didn't know where to begin. Still wondering, he hitched a ride to Lubbock, Texas, in the early spring.

As the grand entry was going out of the arena and the first string of bucking horses were being run into the chutes, Chris was out back, stretching and making ready for his ride. He had always spent a great deal of time getting mentally psyched up for a ride, blowing and pumping, breathing hard, and so on. Now, he noticed World Champion Clyde Vamvoras a few chutes down from himself. Clyde was leaning casually on the chute gate, chewing, spitting, and laughing with a group of other cowboys. He seemed to be getting ready for a trip to the zoo rather than a trip on a bucking horse.

"Now, how in the heck can a guy do that?" Chris asked himself. "He just seems so loose and cool."

A few minutes later, Clyde rigged up his horse, slid down on him and nodded his head. Inside the arena, he "turned on the gas" and made one heck of a ride, well deserving of the introduction the announcer had given the reigning champ. Chris just shook his head, not really understanding how anybody could be so relaxed and yet do so well.

After the ride, Chris watched Clyde walk back behind the chutes, hat cocked to one side, and rejoin the little group of cowboys. He could tell by the way Clyde's hands were moving that the champ was telling them what he had done during the ride.

Chris lowered himself down onto his own horse, grabbed his rigging and nodded his head. As the animal blew out, he went into his usual spurring position: laid back, head flopping and loose, eyes closed, and feet grabbing and snapping at the front end. According to the judges, he did all right, but standing behind the chutes afterward, Chris really couldn't remember anything at all about the ride—he could have been turned around backward spurring the animal's rear-end for all he knew.

"How come Clyde remembers every dip, dive and spurlick," Chris mused, "and I can't remember a thing?" He had found out long ago that he could learn a lot by just shutting up and listening when he was around top hands, so he wandered over to the group of cowboys.

Clyde was entered in Mercedes, Texas, the next night, and since Chris was also going he asked him for a ride. Clyde agreed, and a little while later they wandered out to the parking lot and climbed into Clyde's car.

After a few miles they pulled into a small market and Chris bought a bag of cookies and a quart of milk. Clyde came back with a bottle of wine. Their choice of drink symbolized the differences between the green young kid and the veteran pro, both in their ages and in their ideals.

Chris saw rodeo as a sport, and himself as an athlete. He was into health foods and exercise, and generally took good care of himself. Clyde, on the other hand, was from the "old school" of rodeo, where men and times were hard. In Clyde's younger days, rodeo cowboys were much more carefree and gave little consideration to training or conditioning. For their risks, if they were lucky enough to win any money, they spent the night living as if there would be no tomorrow—and for many, there was none.

In the car that night, one man represented the end of an era, the other a new generation and attitude. But as the wine loosened Clyde's tongue, the similarities between the two were also revealed.

Clyde told of how, as a rookie, he had to hitch-hike to rodeos, often walking miles between rides. Carefully he would pack his boots away in his rigging bag and put on an old dusty pair of flats so as not to wear out his only boots. He spoke of rides in stock trucks and with friends, but mostly of the long hours spent on the side of the road with his thumb up in the air. Chris could appreciate what Clyde had gone through, since it mirrored his present situation.

Then, the subject turned to the riding itself, and Chris found parallels between them in this area as well.

"Shoot," Clyde began, "back in those days, I couldn't tell you, once the ride was over, whether I had spurred him in the neck, in the belly, or in the butt. All I knew was I had tried as hard as I could."

Clyde went on to explain how he finally overcame the problem, and since this was exactly what was giving him trouble, Chris listened intently to every word.

"I just had to wake up, ya know, be more aware of what was going on underneath of me." Clyde waved a hand in the darkened interior of the car as he spoke to add emphasis to his words. "I had to open my eyes and force myself to start thinking of what he was doing, and what I was going to do about it."

Chris slowly realized that he had never really paid any attention to what the *horse* was doing, only to his own spurring. He had never tried to anticipate the next jump.

"Well, once I began to become more aware of what they were doing,' Clyde finished, "by watching them and getting a feel for them, my riding improved tremendously." Chris filed this information away and vowed to give it a try at Mercedes.

As the evening wore on, the two talked of everything from religion and politics, to wild times and wilder women. It was an evening that would long stand out in the mind of the impressionable young LeDoux.

At the Mercedes rodeo, Chris made an effort to watch and be aware of the jumping, bucking, diving mass beneath him and just let his spur-ride take care of itself. He also tried to relax a little, and in doing so was able to feel each twist and turn, and to picture exactly what the horse was doing at each moment. It was like starting all over again, finding a whole new world opening up to him. He didn't place in the money at Mercedes, but he felt so good about the new technique that it turned out to be one of his most significant rodeos.

After Mercedes, Clyde and Chris headed back toward Clyde's home near Wichita Falls, Texas. Chris asked to be dropped at the airport there, and he bade a fond farewell to Clyde just before the champ sped off down the road.

Chris had entered Edmonton, Alberta, and bought a ticket from Wichita Falls to Edmonton. After allowing for fees to enter the rodeo, he would arrive in Canada with exactly $3.10 in his pockets. Chris knew it was time to start winning again or else it would be a long, hungry walk home. Once in Edmonton, he bumped into Witch Holman and Jim Smith, and they invited him to sleep on the floor of their room. He gladly accepted.

Chris drew a horse called Sad Sam, and with his new technique, he spurred him into second place. The $350 check could not have been more welcome. He immediately paid back some of the small debts he had accrued from borrowing a few dollars here and there from cowboy friends and made a few loans to those who had "tapped out" and not placed in the money. This was fairly common: the winners shared their spoils, knowing that next week it might be themselves who were down.

Things were starting to roll Chris's way. Back at Wichita Falls, he drew up well and won first place. It was his first RCA victory, and the trophy buckle was a particular source of pride for the young rookie.

As the summer months unfolded, the rodeos became an endless string of bucking horses and hamburgers, iodine and whiskey, rodeo queens and two-steps. Chris maintained his conservatism throughout most of the partying, but he was usually there somewhere, and having just as much fun as any of the drunken cowboys, sticking with his Copenhagen and an occasional beer.

Gladewater, Texas, proved to be a memorable rodeo for Chris. It was a two-head rodeo, and the night before the first go-around, he and a few other cowboys gathered in an apartment in Dallas, listening to John Quintana tell about his bull-riding strategy for the following day.

"Well boys," John began with a gleam in his eyes, "you all know I drew that V-61 bull. They say nobody's ever ridden him, and he even killed one old boy a few years ago." He looked around, making sure he had everyone's attention. "Well, I'm gonna just knee way up on him and push down hard with m' arm." He grabbed at an imaginary rope and illustrated his technique. "Then just ride 'im through the storm. Then, I'll get off and boot him on the rump on his way out of the arena."

Everyone laughed. V-61 was the top bull, belonging to Bill Minick, and he had never been ridden in an RCA rodeo. It was rumored that Bill bought him from a small regional stock contractor after the bull had killed a contestant at an amateur rodeo. Every bull rider had thoughts about that bull, and about the glory of being the first to ride the beast.

The next day, Chris made an excellent ride and won the first go-around in the bareback riding. As he packed up his gear after the event, he noticed Quintana getting ready for the bull riding and, remembering the story from the previous night, Chris called over to him.

"Hey John, don't forget to kick him on the rump when he leaves the arena!" Everyone laughed. With a soft drink in hand, he and his friends watched the remainder of the rodeo.

Finally, the bull riding event came around, and everyone was eager to see John Quintana and V-61. Naturally, they held back the star performer until last, then built him up with an introduction that would make a mother proud . . . V-61's mother, that is. The cowboy just got mentioned in the by-line; the real star was that unconquered bull.

John nodded his face and the gate swung open. In the bull riding, there is no requirement to "start him out" or to mark him, as in the bareback riding and saddlebronc riding, nor do you have to spur, although a rider will receive extra points if he does. The bull riding is mainly a contest of strength and endurance between a 150-pound man and a 2000-pound bull.

True to his word, John kneed up high onto the bull, giving himself a tight center of balance, and forced his riding arm down hard, which pushed his chest back. On his first jump out, the massive bull kicked the back of the chute, throwing its head low. Twisting just slightly as it landed, V-61 kicked the gate itself on the second jump, smashing it onto the adjoining chute. True to its reputation, the bull rose up high in the front. As the front starts down, a bull will kick high and hard with the back feet, often causing a rider to lose sight of the shoulders as he is unceremoniously dumped over the front end or smashed onto the horns. By kneeing way up and pushing on the rope, as he had said he would do, John kept himself back and the shoulders in sight. With each jump, the roaring of the crowd grew louder.

V-61 turned back to the right, trying to dislodge the unwelcome rider, with no success. The animal had never carried a rider this long before in its entire life and was none too pleased about it. It jumped and kicked ever higher, spinning to the right. Somewhere in the middle of this storm, the buzzer sounded. To most, including John, the sound was lost in the din of the crowd. He continued to ride the brute for a few more seconds until he was finally ripped loose and flung to the ground.

The bull headed straight for the catch-pen gate as the crowd went completely wild. Hats were flying everywhere in exaltation. As the bull passed Bill Minick, the contractor threw his hat at the defeated beast, thoroughly disgusted.

"This is incredible, ladies and gentlemen," came the voice from the P.A. "The judges have awarded John Quintanna ninety-four points for the spectacular ride you all just witnessed. . . ."

John let loose a big whoop. The crowd was again on its feet, cheering for the hero in the arena.

As he got near the chutes, Chris heard someone call out to John, "Yeah, but I didn't see you kick him on the rump!" Everyone laughed—especially John.

The next day Chris again placed first in the go-around, handily wrapping up the average and another RCA trophy buckle. It was a real boost to his self-confidence.

After Gladewater, Chris began to rise steadily in the standings, until finally, at Rapid City, South Dakota, Hank Abbey walked up to him and laid a current copy of the *ProRodeo Sports News* in front of him.

"You made the paper, kid," he said with a reserved smile.

Chris looked in disbelief; there it was in black and white. He was in the number fifteen slot—the bottom of the list, but he had made it into print. He gave out a whoop. "Now if I can just hang in there, I'll make the National Finals Rodeo in Oklahoma City!"

A second-place win in the average at Pendleton, and the large check that came with it, clinched Chris's NFR hopes. He would go to the National Finals that year as a rookie. Witch Holman, also a rookie that year, qualified in the saddlebroncs. Chris ended up in twelfth place overall in the standings before the Finals.

He hitched a ride to Oklahoma City from Chicago with Myrtis Dightman. Having been there before, Myrtis was an experienced hand as far as Chris was concerned, and he hoped to learn a lot from him. But he found rodeo was not the only field of expertise on which the bull rider could offer advice:

"Young, single rookie like you," Myrtis began, "shouldn't have no trouble at all!"

Chris looked at him quizzically. "What do you mean?" he asked, thinking Dightman was still talking about rodeo.

"Women, man, women!" Myrtis explained as a grin spread across his face. You work it just right and you'll have a dozen of them before the last go-around."

Chris was fascinated that anyone could think of women at the National Finals and still have enough energy left to ride. Not wanting to let Myrtis see through him, though, he just smiled and nodded his head. Secretly, he knew his thoughts would be filled with bucking horses right up to the last whistle in the tenth go-around, and there'd be no women to distract him.

Finally, across the flat plains of Oklahoma, the lights of the city began to twinkle and glow on the distant horizon. A knot began to twist inside Chris's stomach and worked its way up into his throat. Myrtis could sense the apprehension in the young cowboy and placed an understanding hand on his shoulder. "Take it one horse at a time, kid, and you'll do just fine."

Chris smiled at him, still unable to speak, and nodded his head. Somewhere among those distant lights there twinkled a shiny trophy buckle, one that would have his name on it if he could just take Oklahoma City by storm. He gazed out at the starlit sky. "One horse at a time."

Chapter 10

National Finals

A rodeo's just a rodeo, after riding several years
From ol' Cheyenne to Houston, they never cause too much
  fear.
But let me tell you about one that will chill your very soul.
It happens in December, when it's snowin' and it's cold.
In Oklahoma City there's a building of concrete,
It's where the toughest stock and men will gather and compete.
The points have all been tallied and the stock has all been
  brought.
We've got just two more hours, 'cause it starts at eight o'clock.

It's the Finals, the NFR, the "Series" of the sport.
Hey rookie, can you take ten head, have you got the heart?
You think you're a tough cowboy—we'll find out in the end,
When that final whistle blows and the stock's all in the pen.

The coliseum's quiet, except for the sounds
Of cowboys getting ready, and the workmen of the grounds.
The cowboys ask each other what each other's got—
"Did you draw ol' Necklace, or pluck old Double-Ought?"
The tension now is mounting and the crowd starts pouring in,
A shiver goes all through me, like from a cold, cold wind.
I hear the horses comin' runnin' down the alleyway,
They're snortin' and a blowin' as they shut the sliding gates.

We had too much time a while ago, but not enough time now,
The Anthem is now over, the grand entry's going out.
I sit there on my bronc—I'm ready and I wait,

I hear a chute gate open, so I look out through the gate.
A horse comes boiling out and blows up at the roof,
And then there comes another, kicking like a curly wolf.
I hear the chute boss holler, through the yelling crowd,
He says, "There's one ahead of you, so you'd better get
   screwed down."

I nod my head, I'm in a daze, the horse goes boiling out,
I run my spurs into his neck and then I drag 'em out.
My mind is in a blur, my eyes are seeing red,
The flank catch slams into my back, his rump bangs on my
   head.
From somewhere in the background I can hear the buzzer
   sound,
My hand's jerked from the rigging and I crash into the
   ground.
I stumble to my feet as I stagger to the wall,
I wonder to myself, "Is it really worth it all?"

Chris LeDoux (Wyoming Brand Music),
from **Rodeo Songs Old and New**

Chris and Myrtis Dightman wheeled into Oklahoma City as soft fingers of pink and yellow light began to color the dark gray dawn. They went downtown and got a room but were to excited to go to bed. Instead, they drove down to the fairgrounds for a look at the building in which the National Finals Rodeo would be held. Chris had been here in the fall for a regular rodeo, but now the massive concrete structure seemed to take on a more ominous look.

Although it was still quite early, the rodeo office was already open, so the two went in and paid their fees. The rodeo secretary gave them their contestant numbers and instructions for the pre-rodeo ceremonies and grand-entry rehearsals.

"Grand-entry rehearsals?" Chris exclaimed as they walked away from the office. "I haven't ridden in a grand entry all year, let alone one that had to have a rehearsal."

Myrtis just shook his head. "Welcome to the National Finals, kid," he said.

Chris decided that since he had some time to kill, he would do some shopping at a few of the famous Oklahoma City Western wear and tack outlets, and bought himself a new pair of riding boots and a new cinch. He had always had nightmares about his cinch breaking at the NFR, so he wanted to make sure it was brand new heading into the first go.

Later, Chris stopped to say hello to his parents, who had come down from Tennessee to watch him in his first Finals bid. They were staying at the Holiday Inn, a world apart from the decrepit old Black Hotel in which Chris was registered. Where he would sleep, however, was the furthest thing from his mind, as the first go-around drew near.

After leaving the Holiday Inn, Chris headed back to the rodeo grounds. All along the way, thoughts of what he had always pictured the NFR to be kept racing through his mind. He remembered what Clyde Vamvoras had told him about the NFR just a few months earlier: "I've seen a lot of guys go there, expecting to fill their pockets, and not win a dime, then they'd have to borrow money to get to Denver the next month."

Chris knew it was going to be a tough rodeo. He would be up on ten head of stock in nine days, and that alone was more punishment than most people could take. Chris didn't know what to expect of himself, but he figured if he could win a few dollars and make a good showing in his first NFR, it would be well worth the while. Of course, the dream was still nagging at him—to win that Finals buckle. But he knew, like most rookies, he'd have a lot of other Finals to go to if he didn't make it this year.

Back at the rodeo grounds, Chris was swept up in a whirlwind of activities, from photograph sessions to grand-entry rehearsals. The next few hours seemed to race past, drawing him ever nearer to the first gate. The magnitude of this rodeo was beginning to make its impression on him.

Finally, a few hours before showtime, the rodeo secretary posted the draw for the first go-around. Chris had visions of

drawing horses like Necklace or Three Bars, but when he finally elbowed his way up to the board he found he was to mount
a horse called Sunburnt, from Sutton's rodeo string. Chris
had seen the horse earlier in the year and remember he liked
to duck and swoop a bit but could really buck. It wasn't
Necklace, but Chris knew he'd have his hands full.

At the National Finals Rodeo, all of the top hands in professional rodeo are represented in their events. What many
people do not realize is that the top livestock is also featured.
From literally hundreds of bucking horses and bulls, only the
best are chosen, to provide the most explosive combinations
at every performance. Awards are given to the owners of these
chosen few, and of the elite group of livestock, one animal
is later chosen in each event as the NFR "Bucking Horse"
or "Bucking Bull of the Year." It is a very prestigious award,
and difficult to come by, so the stock contractors make every
effort to put forth their finest offerings each year.

Even though the first performance was still nearly two hours
away, Chris went over to the main building and walked up
the alleyway into the arena. The domed structure was quiet
and brightly lit. Stopping in front of the bucking chutes, he
scanned the bleachers, empty now but for a few maintenance
people sweeping or setting up seats. The big gray and yellow
structure seemed to crackle with an electric charge, a harbinger
of the excitement yet to come. Chris stood there, mesmerized
and soaked in the feeling of the building, trying to picture the
packed stands and the colorfully dressed pick-up men—all the
things he would see in a few short hours.

Behind him he could hear the sounds of a group of cowboys
milling around behind the chutes. Perhaps they were old
veterans, like Clyde Vamvoras, Royce Smith and John Edwards; or first-timers, like Chris, T.J. Walter or Jay Himes.
It's been said, "Every cowboy is a champion until the chute
gate is opened for the first time." Every contestant here had
paid his dues, and any one of them was capable of winning;
they were all on the same level—for a few short hours, at least.

Chris could feel the adrenalin start to flow and his stomach began tying itself in knots. He walked back behind the chutes with the others and joined in the joking and bantering going on between the cowboys, seeking to relieve the tension building within all of them.

The sport of rodeo, while ostensibly pitting cowboy against cowboy in any given event, actually breaks down to a one-on-one match between man and beast. Every cowboy going down the road knows his competition is the horse, bull or steer that he's drawn; it's how well he handles that animal that determines who walks away with a check. For this reason, cowboys seldom see each other as adversaries or opponents. Instead of being pushed apart by the feelings of rivalry many professional athletes have for their opposition, cowboys are drawn together by the common bond they all share: the danger and thrill of head-on competition with wild livestock. It creates a tie not unlike that shared by men who have faced combat or been through a major disaster together.

Behind the chutes, they compare notes about stock, each telling the others what to expect, if he is familiar with a particular animal. They help each other with equipment and injuries, and make last minute repairs or loans—all for someone who will be riding in the same event, for the same purse. A cowboy is never left wanting for long; if he is in need, someone behind the chutes will have just what he lacks, and is willing to share it gladly. It is this very kinship which keeps many an old cowboy going down the road for years after he has lost his competitive edge. Even if they cannot compete, they will be out back, lending a hand and doing whatever they can for those who can.

Such was the feeling at the NFR in those short hours before the first go-around. The older, experienced hands answered questions and told the rookies and newcomers what to expect and how to keep their cool. They all went over equipment for the umteenth time, making sure everything was just right. Some stretched out casually and relaxed, keeping more to themselves, while others laughed and whooped it up in a small crowd. Everyone had his own release valve, and used it. But they all gathered strength and confidence from each other.

Soon, the arena began to fill with spectators, trickling in at first, then surging through the gates in a massive throng, filling the over ten thousand seats to capacity. The noise from the audience became almost deafening, but behind the chutes, the cowboys were scarcely aware of the din. They had settled down to their individual routines of pre-rodeo preparations: applying rosin to gloves, saddles and ropes; strapping on spurs and chaps; checking cinches and latigos for wear; stretching and loosening up physically; drawing mental pictures of their rides; and spurring the air to build up the adrenalin and concentration. In making sure no detail was overlooked, they generally checked each item two or three times. After all, this was no ordinary rodeo—this was the National Finals.

As in most rodeos, the bareback riding would be the first event of the evening. But unlike most rodeos, the bareback riders would be required to ride in the grand entry. This provided a major logistical problem, since they *should* be behind the chutes getting rigged up. It also provided an extra hardship for cowboys like Chris, who liked to get mentally psyched-up before a ride. Instead of pacing back and forth, creating a picture in his mind of his ride, he would be put in the arena on a saddle horse, waving to the crowd.

For expediency, the fourteenth- and fifteenth-place bareback riders in the standings would be excused from the grand entry to get rigged up and ready to ride when the arena was clear. Everyone else had to exit the arena, dismount, turn their horses over to a hostler, race back behind the chutes, pull up their riggings, adjust chaps, spurs and straps, get gloved-up, then mounted and ready—all in the space of two rides, if you happened to be the number-three man.

Before mounting for the grand entry, the first string of bareback horses were run into the chutes and the cowboys placed their riggings on their mounts loosely. Chris had no trouble spotting his yellow horse, and his heart sank when he saw it standing in chute three.

"Oh no," he said to himself, knowing the pressure would really be on him to hurry. He looked around for Witch Holman, who was entered in the saddlebroncs, an event placed well after the barebacks. Chris asked him to be around the chute after grand entry, knowing he'd need some help if he was to be ready in time. Witch quickly assured Chris he'd be there.

In a few minutes, they were running out behind the main building to the small warm-up arena, which would be used as a staging area for the grand entry. Chris grabbed the reins of a dapple gray mare and vaulted into the saddle. The cool December night was refreshing and served to clear a few heads. Chris could hear muffled sounds from within the building, highlighted by a voice he knew would be the announcer, Clem McSpadden, although he couldn't understand any of the words. The Finals seemed to be a world away.

The arena director ran around calling out instructions to everyone, ordering them to line up alphabetically according to states. It was just as they had rehearsed, and soon the riders from Alabama were charging up the alleyway into the arena. Being from Wyoming, Chris was at the very back of the line and glad for the delay. He was still struggling with his nerves, as were most of the rookies—and even some of the old timers.

Finally, the director signaled for Chris to "come-a-riding," and he lightly brushed the gray's belly with his spurs. He became aware of the gradually increasing noise level as they approached the alleyway, but he was concentrating on the gently loping horse underneath him and not paying much attention to the building ahead.

Suddenly, they were in the alleyway, and then out into the arena. The lights and noise exploded around Chris, and he was momentarily shaken, but he quickly regained his composure and continued the ride as he had rehearsed it.

In all his imaginings, he had not painted a picture as vivid as the one before him now. While the introductions were being made and the Anthem played, Chris looked out into the crowd, absently searching for familiar faces. He knew Bonnie and Al would be out there, as well as some of his other friends. Witch Holman's dad was also down from Wyoming. He began to relax a bit, standing quietly during "The Star Spangled Banner," but then realized this was his cue to get ready for the date he had made with Sunburnt in chute three.

Sitting in the saddle, he tried to get a mental picture of exactly what he would do as they left the arena so when the time came he could move as quickly as possible. Suddenly, the crowd began cheering, and Chris knew the Anthem was over; it was time to leap into action.

He was one of the last riders to leave the arena. Sensing he was already behind, he vaulted from the saddle of the gray, not bothering to turn her over to a hostler. "Heck, she ain't goin' very far," he thought as he raced to the fence.

Witch was right behind him, his horse also having been turned loose, and as Chris grabbed for his riding glove, T.J. Walter burst out into the arena on a horse named Sunset. Chris froze for just a second, watching the horse jump and kick, then circle to the right, with T.J. spurring wildly. He shook his head, thrust his hand into his glove, and jumped for the chute.

Sonny Linger, the chute boss, hollered over to Chris, "You're third, cowboy, pull 'er down."

Chris was relieved to see Witch on the arena side of the chute with a latigo in his hands, making ready to tighten up the cinch. Chris tied-off his glove thong and slid down onto the horse.

"Pull 'er, Witch," he said quietly, as he held the rigging centered on the withers. Witch complied, snugging up the cinch to Chris's satisfaction.

Chris heard a chute gate bang open, and he looked up to see Bobby Mayo high-dive into the arena.

"Dang," he said softly, looking at the way Bobby's horse was bucking. It suddenly dawned on Chris just how elite these horses were—there wasn't a bad one in the string.

He grabbed his glove thong with his teeth and free hand
and tied it off securely. Then he ran his hand into the rigging
handle, working it into just the right position.

"You ready, Chris?" asked Sonny from the arena, with a
hand on the top of the gate.

"Boy, am I," Chris thought eagerly, sliding up into his rigging and getting his feet into position. Somewhere off in the
distance, Chris was vaguely aware of his name being announced by Clem McSpadden and the deafening roar of the
crowd being worked into a frenzy by the artful announcer and
the explosive roughstock.

Chris nodded his head and rolled into the arena with Sunburnt. The horse ducked to the right, then switched back to
the left, but Chris was ready for him and was in perfect position. He lay back and started a smooth spur-ride, as the horse
evened out into a strong, rythmic bucking action. He turned
back gradually to the right again, and Chris felt so confident,
he was certain a stick of dynamite exploding in his back pocket
wouldn't be powerful enough to separate him from that animal. The whistle sounded, and Chris grabbed the rigging with
his free hand and sat upright. The pick-up men moved in skillfully and maneuvered Sunburnt in between them at a full run.
Chris grabbed the cantleboard of one man and pulled himself
off the wild horse, while the other man reached down and
released the flank strap from the still-kicking animal.

As Chris reached the ground, he could feel his knees begin
to tremble from the release of tension. He staggered to the
fence to collect his strength while the judges called out his
score. It was pretty good, and Chris sighed with relief as the
crowd cheered wildly.

Always at the NFR, and especially for a rookie, the first
ride is the most important ride of the rodeo. It will set the
pace for the entire contest. If you make a good ride right off,
it builds your confidence and self-assuredness. If you buck-
off, miss one out, or just do poorly, you spend the next nine
horses trying to catch up from a position of weakened self-
confidence. It makes it very difficult to come back.

Chris had cleared that first obstacle and had scored well. In fact, he ended up in third place for the go-around, behind Gary Tucker on Moonshine and John Edwards on Paper Doll. Watching the remainder of the round, Chris was amazed by the amount of effort that went into every ride. People he had gone down the road with all year were riding better than Chris had ever seen before; but then, he supposed, that was what the Finals was all about.

After the bareback event, Chris went back behind the chutes to help Witch get rigged up for the saddlebronc riding event. Holman had drawn a horse named Major Reno, the scourge of the RCA, having been ridden only a few times all year. Witch was eager to try the infamous brute, but apprehensive as well. As he settled into the saddle, he placed his feet out into the front, just above where he would "start" the horse out of the chute.

Like the bareback riding, saddlebronc riding rules require a rider to set his spurs firmly into the horse's neck, in front of the break in the shoulder, on the first jump out of the gate. Usually, riders will hold this "mark" for two full jumps, both to make sure they started him out properly, and to get the feel of the bucking animal beneath them so they can fall into rhythm with the bronc.

Unlike the bareback rider, a saddlebronc rider has a hack rein to hold onto and an Association Saddle to sit in. The free hand cannot touch the rider, horse or equipment, and the spur-ring action involves sweeping the feet from the neck to the flank, with the better riders ending the spur-lick as high as the cantleboard of their saddle. This fore-and-aft spurring action is timed to flow with the horse's bucking action so the spurs will be forward when the animal's front feet are on the ground and swept back when the animal is jumping forward, with its front feet up in the air.

John's strategy for riding the legendary Major Reno was simply to hold his spurs in the front end for at least two jumps, long enough for the horse to settle into a solid bucking pattern, before committing himself to the spur-ride. By clamping tightly with his spurs over the point of the shoulders, his thighs would be firmly held in the swells of the saddle, thus providing maximum stability during the initial leap into the arena.

Gritting his teeth, he locked his legs tightly against the horse and held his bronc rein high in the air. The only thing he forgot to do was nod his head.

"You want the gate, Witch?" Chris asked, sensing Holman was ready.

Breaking his concentration for just a second, Witch glanced at Chris, realizing his omission, and dipped his head. The horse, true to form, reared out high, dancing on his back feet and pawing at the air with his front feet. Witch was laid back and nearly vertical to the ground, hanging by his well-placed feet, which were firmly in front of the horse's shoulder.

From that spectacular introduction, Major Reno dove into the arena and landed on his front feet with a jarring impact that sent Witch slamming into the swells, but his feet were still locked out over the front. The horse planted his feet and fired straight up into the air, swiveling slightly to the left, showing his belly to the crowd. Hitting the ground, he lurched forward in a powerful dive, which was followed by a nearly vertical thrust with his back feet, kicking high into the air. Witch still refused to move from his position.

With Witch's feet set into the horse's neck as if they were welded in place, the horse leapt into the air again. This time, however, the power was too great, and as the horse started back down, the cowboy was left, for an instant, in the air at the top of the dive. The power of the animal had ripped the swells of the saddle right out from under Witch, and with his spurs still holding tightly to the animal's neck, he swiveled over the front of the beast and was unceremoniously dumped into the arena dirt, head first. Miraculously, the charging animal neither stepped on nor kicked the fallen rider, but there was immeasurable damage to Holman's pride. As he dusted himself off and moved back behind the chutes, Chris met him with a smile and a warm pat on the back.

Knowing what was going through Holman's mind, Chris spoke: "There ain't no shame in bucking off of that horse, Witch," he said sincerely. "He's humbled some of the best this year, and he'll humble a few more before he's through."

Witch looked up at him, knowing he was right, and allowed a tight smile to escape his lips. "Thanks, partner," he said.

As each go-around was recorded in the history books, Chris continued to ride consistently well and scored at each performance. In the sixth go-around, he drew a horse named Honest Abe and won first place. It moved him into the lead in the average. Since he entered the rodeo in the number twelve slot, he was really pleased with himself—and rightly so. It isn't often a rookie has the stamina and character to make a great first showing at the NFR, but Chris was doing just that.

After the ninth horse, only Chris and John Edwards had qualified on every ride, and Chris had a comfortable lead going into the last go-around. All of the other competitors had bucked off, missed one out, or in some other way fouled their rides in at least one go-around. Because of this, Chris needed only a forty-seven point ride to win the Finals Buckle.

His confidence bolstered by his excellent performances up to this point, Chris was beginning to believe he might actually win the average. His dream was just a spur-ride away. Even Al and Bonnie were beginning to believe Chris was going to win it, and Al reserved a meeting room at the Holiday Inn on Saturday night for a little party.

Just a few friends were invited. Chris managed to down a fair amount of whiskey and happily soaked up the attention directed toward him as the average leader. It was definitely the high point of his first pro year.

The next afternoon, Chris went into the secretary's office to check the draw for the last go. T.J. Walter was sitting in the room, and seeing Chris, he offered, "You've got Sunset, Chris."

Looking quickly at the sheets, Chris realized T.J. had had the horse in the first go-around, and he asked his old college teammate just what he could expect.

"He's a good one, but I had him in the first go and missed him out," answered T.J. thoughtfully, going over the ride again in his mind, making sure nothing significant slipped by him. "He'll blow out of there, and then drop ... so you'd better have it on your mind."

Chris thought back to that first, frantic go-around when he was in the third chute, and he remembered thinking how well the horse had bucked. He thanked T.J. for the information and headed back out.

"Shoot," Chris mused to himself, "I haven't had any trouble marking anything out all year. This is going to be a piece of cake." He thought about how he would look walking around with that Finals Buckle strapped to his belly.

Finally the big moment came and Chris lowered himself down onto the horse. He knew he would have to try a little harder at the gate and vowed to really bear down and reach for that mark, then lay back and just gas it. He knew he only needed forty-seven points, but it was not his style to "safety-up" and take the easy way out. He would ride this horse just as if it were his first horse of the rodeo.

He nodded his head, and the horse dropped sharply out of the chute, stumbling once, then launching into a kicking, rearing fit. Chris rode him well and felt good as the whistle sounded. He reached up with his free hand, pulling himself up, to wait for the pick-up man to set him on the ground.

Suddenly, the P.A. system blared, "Oh no," said Clem, "you're gonna hate this..."

Chris already hated it—he could feel his stomach drop inside himself.

"... the judges say he missed his mark, ladies and gentlemen. A no-score for this Wyoming cowboy ...."

Chris felt like rolling off of the horse, getting hung up and being dragged to death underneath it. Of course, the pick-up

men whisked him safely away before he could do that, but
he felt terrible. T.J. Walter's words came back to haunt him:
"... you'd better have it on your mind...."

In the minutes after the ride, a multitude of images raced
through his mind: the buckle, the ticker-tape parades, the
headlines he had imagined, all were shattered dreams now.
He hung his head in shame, although in reality he had performed exceptionally well, and had nothing to be ashamed of.

Chris finished up in third place in the average, with John
Edwards winning the buckle. Including all his day-money and
his average-money check, he had earned over $3400 at the
Finals, so it was by no means a waste of time. He had earned
a name and a reputation as well, so he was no longer considered a "rookie kid." But the Finals Buckle had slipped
through his fingers, and coming so close had made him want
it even more than ever.

As the crowd of spectators began shuffling toward the
doors, Chris looked up into the bright lights of the arena.
"Next year."

Chapter 11

Tight Levis and Yellow Ribbons

I was born and raised in the red clay hills of Texas,
In the land where the grass gets only beer-can tall.
It's where I learned to cuss and fight, and chew Brown Mule
  tobacco,
Fixed windmills, 'fore I was five years old.

I've rode every head of stock, from the Gulf to Kansas City,
And running wild is all I've ever known.
But this cowboy's got a weakness—tight Levis and yellow
  ribbons,
And there's somethin' 'bout 'em I can't leave alone.

Tight Levis and yellow ribbons make a cowboy swim a river
That before he jumps he knows is way too wide.
And they'll make him throw a saddle on a bronc he's never
  seen—
And one he knows he'll never break to ride.

I met her at a rodeo in Douglas, Arizona.
I drawed the rankest horse a man could draw.
Well, I rode him tall, and spurred him high, and when I made
  the whistle
The crowd went wild, but she was all I saw.
That night we had a beer or two with friends of mine from
  Dallas;
She smiled and said she loved a Texas drawl,

I felt like Roy Rogers did in all those cowboy movies,
'Cause I became the hero—got the money, girl and all!
Glen Sutton/Red Steagall (Talo Duro/Rodeo Cowboy Music),
**   from Rodeo and Living Free**

After the 1970 NFR, Chris spent some time with his folks in Tennessee. Even though he hadn't won the Finals Rodeo, he had finally convinced himself that he had a true talent for riding bareback horses and was actually in the same league with those whom he had admired for so many years—men like Clyde Vamvoras, John Edwards, Paul Mayo and Gary Tucker. The time spent with his parents allowed him to collect his thoughts, relax from a hard year, and prepare for the upcoming season.

Having once come so close to winning the Finals Buckle, Chris doubled his resolve to become the World's Champion and decided to increase the number of rodeos that he would enter, thinking this would win him more money and make him more successful. He was soon to learn a valuable lesson about the difference between rodeoing "hard" and rodeoing "smart."

Chris had always heard that if a cowboy was to be a serious contender for the World Title, he would have to get to as many rodeos as was humanly possible. Consequently, in the spring of 1971, he found himself hitching rides, hopping buses or catching airplanes for rodeos all over the country—regardless of his draw, added money or his own physical and mental condition.

He placed in a few shows but made just enough to keep going, never really getting ahead. He found, while his expenses rose dramatically, his winnings did not rise proportionally.

Things reached their hectic peak in late spring, after he finished out of the money at Jasper and Mineral Wells, Texas, and had the same results at Guymon, Oklahoma. Three rodeos in a row and no paycheck had brought Chris close to broke.

To compound his problems, his next rodeo was in Long Beach, California, an expensive plane ride away.

"Where's the nearest airport?" Chris asked Texas bareback rider Jack Ward.

"Airport?" Jack responded with a wry grin. "Where you headed to, Chris?"

"Long Beach, California," Chris replied matter-of-factly.

Jack raised an eyebrow. "Heck, you must've drawed up real good to go that far, huh?"

"Aw, I don't even know what I got, I just know I gotta get on down there and give it a try," Chris answered sheepishly.

Jack slapped his knee and burst out laughing. When he came up for air, he looked at Chris and said, "You're in Guymon, Oklahoma, friend, not some big city. I s'pose you'll have to get yourself a ride down to Amarillo if you really want to get to Long Beach." He was trying hard to control himself. "I can't believe you'd even consider going down there without knowing your draw, pard."

Chris didn't really understand the joke. He figured everybody who was serious about winning the title would be doing exactly what he was doing: going to every rodeo he could. Sure, he'd drawn a few bad ones from time to time, but they all averaged out in the end.

When he got to California, Chris found he had drawn a new horse of Cotton Rosser's that just scattered and ran across the arena; his score was so low he didn't even come close to the money. It was then he'd begun to understand what Jack was laughing about. Nearly broke, Chris knew if he had just taken the time to find out that he had drawn a green horse, he would never have spent the money to fly all the way to California. In the long run, the turn-out fine would have been cheaper.

As the months raced past, Chris spent more time working out ways to rodeo "smart" rather than "hard," recognizing the importance of checking every draw to evaluate the odds. Rodeo is much like a poker game: a lot of folks just play out every hand for the fun of it and don't really care whether they win or lose. A professional gambler, on the other hand, knows the odds of every draw and folds on those inside straights. He knows the chances of making any money on a long-shot are slim to none. A green horse or a known runner was an "inside straight," and Chris found it better and cheaper to fold his hand and pay his fines than to spend all his travel money for nothing.

He also found he had hot and cold streaks, and he performed much better when he was completely healthy. Accepting that on different days he was going to ride differently, he learned to capitalize on it by going just a little harder when he was hot, and laying off for a few days or a week when he was cold, or injured.

Rodeoing smart began to pay off for Chris, and by mid-summer he was back in the middle of the pack and racing toward a top finish for the year. His confidence was up, and he was having a great time. Then, in July, he found himself back in Sheridan, Wyoming, surrounded by old friends. John Forbes, Witch Holman and Chris once again fell in together, and the three decided to ride up to Calgary the day after the competition was finished in Sheridan. But right now there was a good rodeo and a great dance afterwards they all intended to make.

When the bareback riding had ended, Chris went out into the grandstand area to buy himself a soft drink and bumped into Peggy Rhoads, a Kaycee native who had come to Sheridan for the rodeo. Chris had met Peggy a few years earlier but had never asked her out. He had always thought she was very pretty, but had never given himself much of a chance for a date with her. As they talked, Chris noticed how the sunlight shimmered in her golden hair, and how her green eyes sparkled as she laughed at his stories. They talked for quite some time while watching the rest of the rodeo, but soon Chris knew he needed to get back behind the chutes again. Working up his

courage, he asked Peggy if she wanted to go to the rodeo dance
with him.

"Why, that sounds like fun, Chris," she answered sweet-
ly. Chris grinned from ear to ear.

He bade her farwell and floated back behind the chutes.
Nothing anyone could have said to him at that point would
have upset him. He kept checking his watch, waiting for the
evening to roll around.

Finally, the prescribed time arrived, and Chris picked Peggy
up for their first date. It turned out to be the very best rodeo
dance Chris had ever attended. They drank a few beers and
danced the night away, totally lost in each other's company.

The next day, as John, Witch and Chris headed down the
road for Calgary, Chris had the strangest feeling inside, as
though he had left something behind in Sheridan. Usually
when the three of them teamed up, they spent the whole trip
between rodeos talking about wild horses and wilder women,
and telling the kind of stories that make every cowboy sit just
a bit taller in the saddle. But, for Chris, this trip was different.
The stories were still told, but he often found himself staring
vaguely out the window and thinking about the past night.
He had left other women in other cities, many of them friends
still . . . but none had ever affected him like this pretty little
blonde rancher's daughter.

Witch and John noticed their traveling companion was a
little distracted but decided they were still going to have a good
time in Calgary—and Chris would do the same, whether he
wanted to or not!

They checked into a room at the Palacer Hotel and headed
down to the lounge for a beer. Chris, as usual, settled for his
Copenhagen and a soft drink.

Canada at the time was a favorite hide-out for hippies and
draft evaders from the States. The Palacer had its share of
them, as well as cowboys up for the rodeo, not to mention
the more ordinary-type nicely dressed and well-mannered
tourists. It was a motley collection of people, to say the least,
and one that made for some violent altercations.

"Now some folks don't realize, but it's a well known fact: cowboys and hippies ain't never got along."* Chris, Witch and John ended up at a party in the room of a couple of school teachers who had come up from Dallas for the rodeo. Chris discovered the ladies had brought along some wigs, and he got a devilish twinkle in his eyes.

"How would you girls like to help us pull off a pretty good prank?" Chris asked, sliding up close to the table. He went on to outline his plan, and the ladies quickly agreed. Chris, Witch and another cowboy named Bart Brower each put on a wig, unbuttoned their shirts, took off their boots, and slipped a couple of strands of beads around their necks. When they finally looked into the mirror, the cowboys had been totally transformed: before them stood the images of three ersatz hippies.

Everyone at the party was howling at the imitation hippies, and after enduring the laughter for several minutes, the three took their act "on the road." They had decided to try a cameo appearance in the hotel lounge, which was packed with cowboys, most well on their way to a good drunk by this time of the night.

At the main entrance to the lounge, they were stopped by the hostess. She suggested it might not be healthy for them to go into the bar, explaining the hotel could not be responsible for the actions of the cowboys. Chris peeled back his wig just a bit and winked at the young woman, who realized then it was all a gag. She immediately escorted them to a table in the very center of the room.

The "hippies" quickly became the focus of attention as they settled down into their seats. Seeing some of the smiling faces, Chris thought they had been recognized but decided to continue anyway.

Witch pulled out a cigarette paper and stuffed it with some Bull Durham tobacco, rolling it loosly to resemble a marijuana

---

*From "The Cowboy and the Hippie," off the *Wild Horses* album.

cigarette. After showing the "joint" to Chris and Bart, Witch lit it and allowed the thick smoke to curl up around his head.

World Champion Bull Rider Ronnie Rossen and his friend Leonard McCreavey were sitting a few tables away watching the whole scene with disgust. They had both been drinking for a while and weren't feeling any pain, and the sight of the three hippies had begun in them a slow, boiling rage.

As far as Ronnie and Leonard were concerned, the long-hairs had gone too far by smoking what they thought was marijuana. They got up together and walked over to the table—just as Witch handed the cigarette to Chris. The bar became deathly quiet as Ronnie put his big, gnarled hands on the table and bent down to look Chris straight in the eye.

"Hey boy, what's that stuff you're smokin'?" he asked Chris menacingly.

Chris was nonchalant. "Here man, give it a try," he said as he offered the cigarette to Ronnie.

Ronnie backed up, blinked, and looked around the room, thus assuring everyone he had no intentions of actually taking a drag off of the joint.

Seeing this reaction, Chris said, "Hey man, why don't you and your friend bug out?"

Ronnie snapped back, "What's that s'posed to mean?"

Chris explained, and when Ronnie caught the meaning, he decided that enough was enough. He reached down with his left hand and grabbed Chris by the hair, with every intention of jerking him to his feet. He had drawn back his huge right fist, preparing to smash the "hippie" right in the nose, when the wig came off in his hand.

Ronnie let out a surprised yelp and dropped the thing like a poisonous snake. His mouth fell open, and he stared at his hand, then looked at the wig where it lay on the floor. Leonard, who was reaching for Witch at the same time Ronnie went at Chris, turned to see what had happened and froze. Without the wig, he instantly recognized Chris and turned to examine the other "hippie" to find out who was really under that hair.

Rossen finally gathered his wits and looked back down at Chris, who was beaming like an October moon. A smile began to spread across the bull rider's face, then laughter billowed up from within him and filled the air. The tension in the room dissolved, and everyone, realizing there would be no fight, went back about their business.

Meanwhile, Leonard had peeled the wig off of Witch and grinned when he recognized the cowboy. Bart took his own wig off, and they all had a good laugh together.

Chris admitted later it had been a darned good gag, but he was sure glad Ronnie had pulled his wig off first, before he let loose with that punch.

Later, Chris wandered out into the streets in his costume and, swinging around a light post, started preaching aloud about the evils of civilization. Soon quite a crowd had gathered—mostly hippies—to listen to him.

"I've been up in the mountains, living off of the land," he began once a crowd had formed. "I tell you, it's the only way to live. We need to break up all of this concrete and steel and give the land back to nature," he added, pointing to the city around him.

His words were greeted by choruses of "Right on, man," and "Far out." One old man in a business suit was not so impressed and told Chris he was quite happy with things just the way they were, and threatened to rip off LeDoux's head if he kept on creating a stir.

Chris went back inside the hotel and soon reappeared, looking like a cowboy again, to join Witch and John. They wandered around the city and partook of some of the festivities which rocked the town from one end to the other during Rodeo Days. But through it all, the little green-eyed blonde from Kaycee kept creeping back into Chris's mind.

He didn't ride very well at the rodeo and felt that his lack of concentration was partly to blame. He hoped the out-of-touch feeling would pass, but it turned into something he just couldn't shake. After several poor showings, he could tell he was definitely in a slump, so he decided the best course of action would be a week off—in Kaycee, naturally!

Summertime in Kaycee provides an idyllic setting for a young couple to fall in love. Chris and Peggy spent hours together enjoying the splendor of the land, swimming in the river or sharing a popsicle in the shade of a cottonwood tree. There were nights spent dancing and romancing, and hours cuddling beneath a magnificent Wyoming sky. It was as if the angels had gotten together and decided to create the perfect time and place for two young people to meet and become forever intertwined with each other's lives.

The week was over far too quickly for Chris, but from that time forth, he made it a point to "swing by" Kaycee several times a month for visits, even though he and Peggy still had not made any actual commitment to each other.

Often, while hitch-hiking down the road between rodeos, Chris would imagine she was out on a date with another cowboy. He could just picture her flashing green eyes and hear her sweet voice as she talked or laughed at another man's jokes. It nearly made him crazy.

After failing to place at Sidney and Terry, Chris was feeling particularly despondent. He couldn't concentrate on the horses because he kept thinking of a certain girl. He wasn't ready to get seriously involved, since he was always broke and on the road; on the other hand, he really did like Peggy, and figured if a fellow had to settle down with a woman, she'd be the perfect professional's wife. Then he'd think about her going out with someone else and his whole mood would shift again. Sometimes just hearing the popular Freddie Hart song "Easy Loving" on the radio would be enough to set him to pining.

The next few weeks dragged by for the lovesick cowboy, and finally Chris decided not to fight it any more: he moved in with Witch Holman's folks on their ranch outside of Kaycee in late August.

In October, the two sweethearts talked Bud Rhoads, Peggy's father, into letting her go along with Chris to a rodeo in Bismarck, North Dakota. She piled into the car with Chris and several of the guys and they headed out. Everyone soon learned it was different having a woman along: they had to watch their cussing and belching, and they didn't tell too many "wild women" stories. They did manage to re-tell some of their classic "wild horse" stories, however, often making the horses meaner and bigger with the retelling—much to each other's delight, as they had already heard the stories in their original versions.

Chris also felt strange at the rodeo, spending his time up in the bleachers while all of his friends were down behind the chutes having a good time. He realized then that even if he loved Peggy—and he knew he did—having her at rodeos was going to spell some drastic changes in rodeo life as he knew it.

Chris tried explaining this in a way that Peggy would understand, and let him slip off with his buddies for a while—but she wasn't about to let him sneak off. She had driven hundreds of miles to be with him, and all of the explaining in the world wasn't going to make right what Chris was proposing to do. Reluctantly, he stayed in the grandstands.

As she snuggled up close to him and pressed her hand into his, he decided it wasn't *all* bad, having a lady along for the ride. But as the season progressed, there were difficulties with the relationship, and adjustments had to be made on both sides. Usually these were not too serious, but in the autumn Chris and Peggy had a major falling out.

Chris had again qualified for the NFR, but due to their rift, he left Peggy behind in Kaycee and went to Oklahoma City by himself.

He started off fairly well in the first two go-arounds but missed one out in the third round, putting him out of the running for the buckle. Chris actually felt somewhat relieved, after the big disappointment he'd suffered the previous year, and resolved to take each of the next go-arounds one at a time, go for the best score he could, and try to get some day money. Deep down inside, he knew that part of the reason he wasn't riding well was being away from Peggy.

Finally, she called him at the hotel. They patched things up over the phone, and the long and the short of it was they figured there wouldn't be any problems they couldn't solve together, so they decided to get married shortly after the NFR.

After the Finals, Chris went to Nashville to spend Christmas with his parents. He broke the news about the wedding to Al as they were sailing in the senior LeDoux's boat. Having never met Peggy, Al thought to try to talk Chris out of it, but it was useless. Al realized Chris was truly in love.

"Good luck, son," he said, clapping Chris on the shoulder. Chris was overjoyed, knowing he had his father's blessing.

Chris and Peggy were married on January 4, 1972, in Casper, Wyoming. John Forbes was Chris's best man at the small civil ceremony; Cindy Rhoads, Peggy's cousin, stood by Peggy.

Afterwards, Mr. and Mrs. Chris LeDoux registered at the Henning Hotel in Casper, an older, quaint hostelry with a small restaurant and lounge on the first floor. As it was still early in the afternoon, the newlyweds went downstairs for something to eat.

Chris picked out a table in the dimly lit eatery, but before the couple could sit down, someone grabbed him and began shaking his hand heartily. Chris squinted in the near-darkness, trying to see just who it was on the other end of his arm.

"Well, I'll be," he said, finally recognizing the features. "Mike Hubble. What the heck are you doing here?"

"Why, me and Gene just come up for a bite to eat," Mike answered, pointing to a cowboy in the corner, who tipped his hat when he noticed the group looking his way. "We share a place here in town. Say, why don't y'all come on over and join us at our table?"

Chris agreed, and soon the four were seated at the table.

"Chris, you remember Gene Walker from your college days here?" said Mike, by way of introduction.

Chris reached out a hand in Gene's direction. "Well, sure I do," he answered. He then introduced his new bride to the two cowboys, who, upon learning of their recent nuptials, insisted the bride and groom come by the house after supper for a drink.

Some time later, Chris and Peggy closed the door to their hotel room and made ready for their first night as husband and wife. Just as Chris slid into bed next to his wife, they heard a muffled metallic clanging noise coming from the hallway. Chris cocked his head, trying to hear better so he could ascertain the origin of the sound, which seemed to be coming from directly outside their door. He looked above the door to the partially opened transom, hoping to see a reflection in the window into the hall.

Suddenly, something snaked through the transom, fell nearly to the floor inside the room and hung limply from the window. Both Chris and Peggy froze, trying to figure out exactly what was going on, when they heard a voice outside in the hall: "Go ahead and turn it on, Gene."

Chris instantly recognized Mike's voice and fired out of bed like a shot. He didn't know what Mike and Gene were up to, but he figured it had to be no good. Before he had taken two steps, the long serpentine object came to life, sputtering and snapping, then flopping around wildly, like a snake stuck in a light socket.

"Holy smokes!" Chris yelled to Peggy, who was still in bed clutching the covers around herself. "They've turned on the firehose!"

Water sprayed everywhere, soaking the small room. Chris threw open the door and ran out underneath the nozzle, soaking himself in the process. He followed the hose down the hallway and quickly turned the water off. Mike and Gene had already disappeared.

Chris rolled the hose into its rack and trudged back down the hall to his room. Opening the door, he surveyed the damage: puddles of water everywhere, curtains and walls soaked—even the bed had a fair amount of moisture.

Peggy, seeing Chris standing in the doorway soaked to the bone, started laughing. He chuckled himself as he turned out the lights.

"What a way to start a marriage, huh?" he said sheepishly as he slid into the wet bed next to Peg. "But it's gonna take a lot more than that old firehose to dampen my spirits tonight!"

Chapter 12

Our First Year

The winter winds were blowin' when we loaded that old truck
With a few things that we had, and all our dreams.
With my new bride here beside me, we headed down the road,
I would show her places and things she'd never seen.
First we went to Denver, Ft. Worth and San Antone,
She cheered me on at every rodeo.
But Houston finally ended, then San Angelo,
I didn't want to tell her, but she knew that we were broke.

Then in California the baby started showin'
And all her clothes were gettin' way too small.
We couldn't spare the money to buy her any new ones,
She just wore my shirt and jeans and didn't mind at all.
And early in the morning we'd wake up by the roadside,
I'd build a fire, and she'd get out the eggs.
She'd cook us up some breakfast, then we'd sit down on the
  grass,
Lord, those were the best meals I guess I ever ate.

She never complained when the winnings didn't come,
She just took it all in stride.
And if I rode good or bit the dust, she was just as proud—
She was happy just bein' by my side.
Now those days are over, and somehow we got ahead.
That little girl I married is still here with me.

We finally got the house we planned down there beside the stream,
And all those old hard times are just cherished memories.

Chris LeDoux (Wyoming Brand Music),
from **Sounds of Rodeo & Country**

The LeDouxs set up housekeeping in a small kitchenette apartment in the Siesta Motel in Kaycee. Peggy took a job in the local cafe as a waitress, and Chris kept busy hunting, fishing, and getting in shape for the first big rodeo of the season at Denver.

Several months before he had gotten married, Chris had teamed up with Witch Holman to buy a new Chevy Suburban, which they dubbed "Rodeo Rose." They each contributed to the down payment and split the payments every month. But after the wedding, Witch told Chris to "just keep the thing" as a wedding present. So, for the first time in his rodeo career, Chris had solid transportation and didn't need to worry about hitching rides any longer.

Because of their financial situation, they decided that Chris would hit the road alone, and Peggy would stay behind to work at the cafe. Neither of the newlyweds was pleased with the arrangement, but Peggy would come along from time to time, and on longer trips she could come for a day or two and then ride back with friends.

After just a few weeks of married life, Chris motored out in Rodeo Rose, headed for Denver. But he soon found out he had too much on his mind to concentrate fully on the horses. He called Peggy every day, and after only three days apart, she hitched a ride to Denver with Curt and Nicki Taylor. The Taylors were only going to be in Denver for a couple of days, and Peggy had arranged to ride back with them as well.

Chris was delighted to see her again and decided things just wouldn't be right unless she was beside him. In a lot of ways, he still felt like a stranger around her, but in other ways she had become part of his being.

"Look, Peg," he stammered after the rodeo had ended. "I've got one hundred and fifteen dollars, and I've got a good horse in Amarillo. Why don't we just take off and go?"

Her eyes lit up, and she readily agreed. Peggy called the cafe and told them she wouldn't be coming back, and together they drove down to Amarillo.

Chris had drawn a horse named Top Out and won the bareback riding event. He pocketed nearly eight hundred dollars for the ride, and the LeDouxs were back in business! They stayed in motels and ate at restaurants, and really enjoyed each other's company. This was a whole new way to rodeo for Chris, and while it was very different from going down the road with "the boys," it certainly had some advantages.

They moved on to Houston, then San Angelo, and Chris placed out of the money at both of those shows. As their pockets emptied, their lifestyle changed accordingly. Chris bought some fishing line and a few hooks, and they camped out by rivers or streams, fishing for their supper. They converted the back of the Suburban into a bed and slept in the truck. It was a little more rugged than the days right after Amarillo, but it was still pretty nice for the young couple.

Chris felt it was doubly important to check out his draw at the next rodeo, since it was all the way out in San Diego, California. He asked J.C. Trujillo about the horse called Southern Pride.

"Shoot, that's a good horse," replied J.C., stroking his chin. "You'd better go get on him."

Chris loaded up the truck and hit the road. They had to drive under fifty m.p.h. all the way from Texas to California, since Rose had developed a terrible shimmy in her front end. On top of that, the tires were worn down nearly to the air. Chris carefully doled out their last few dollars, holding back only enough for entry fees at San Diego.

Their luck held out, as Chris scored eighty-two points and won the bareback riding. He picked up a check for $550, which they promptly cashed. Rodeo Rose got two new tires and her front end adjusted, and they headed out to Phoenix, Arizona. By the end of the rodeo they were nearly broke again, but they didn't mind a bit.

Eventually, they migrated back to Kaycee and laid off for a few weeks. Then it was out to California again, this time to rodeos in Red Bluff, Angel's Camp and Hayward, among many others. After the snow and mud of Wyoming, the warm, green spring of California was a welcome sight.

Since most of the West Coast rodeos were on weekends, weekdays were free for "hanging out." The LeDouxs would usually set up camp in a park somewhere and get in some fishing. Chris even made some crude furniture and utensils out of wood. The high point of each day was a venture to the nearest cafe for a cup of coffee, where they would sip their hot drinks slowly, savoring the peace and tranquility.

Peggy, who was now several months pregnant, had taken to wearing Chris's clothes, since none of hers fit any more. Most mornings, they ate French toast cooked out over an open fire. Chris recorded all these facts in the song "Our First Year," but when his father pointed out that French toast was not ordinarily a poor man's breakfast, he later changed the words to simply "breakfast."

Soon they headed northward, taking in Comanche Village, Eugene, Oregon, and Seattle, Washington, among other Northwest rodeos. At Seattle he earned less than $30, bringing his month's total up to $129. They were really in the basement now, but they decided to try to make it back to Kaycee.

Larry Jordan needed a lift to Montana, so the three of them headed out together. They made it to Montana with no problems, but soon after dropping Larry off in Billings, Chris made a collect call to Nashville.

He had several hundred dollars stashed in an emergency fund in a bank there, and he asked Al to wire it out to them. Naturally, Al agreed to send the money ... but not before he told Chris just exactly what he thought of the younger LeDoux's career choice.

"Aren't you getting tired of kicking the manure around?"
he asked. "You've got a wife now, and soon you're to have
a baby. Look, why don't you two just come on down here?
They have a good art school here, and you can live with us
for a while—until you get squared away."

Chris had never even considered giving up rodeo, but his
father's words really hit home. He had known a baby would
make a big difference in his life, but he had never figured it
would mean giving up the sport. He climbed back into the
truck and told Peg they could pick the money up in the morning. He didn't tell her the rest of the conversation; it was something he would have to think through first.

Chris's slump had much to do with the fact he was drawing up poorly and his confidence was waning. Part of it also
had to do with his family situation and his impending father-
hood. He was worried and distracted.

A few weeks after returning to Kaycee, Chris headed back
out on the road—but this time he went alone. He knew he
would have to travel lightly and cheaply to get to the most
summer rodeos. He figured on picking up a few riders between
rodeos to help cut down on gas money, and he'd eat a lot of
pork-n-beans and bologna. He still didn't like leaving Peggy,
but he knew it was for the best. Now if he could just snap
his cold streak....

Chris went first to Vernon, Texas, and drew a scattering
horse that put him out of the money again. He had never been
at a lower emotional state than he was now. It seemed the
whole world was working against him—but he wouldn't give
up. He entered Jasper, Texas, and got a horse named King
Lear, which he knew to be a good draw.

"Well, you've been telling yourself that this cold streak has
been on account of bad draws," he told himself before the
rodeo. "Now you've got a good one, so if you mess this one
up, it's on nobody's shoulders but your own." Chris knew
he needed a good ride, and he resolved to bear down and give
it his all.

The good Lord must have answered his prayers and helped to set his spurs: Chris won the bareback riding event. Later that day, he ran into Clyde Vamvoras, who knew about his slump and had just learned about Chris winning Jasper. He told Chris, "Well, you just can't keep a squirrel on the ground in timber country."

Chris laughed, but he knew deep inside he had broken the slump. He started feeling good about himself again.

Chris finished out the rest of the summer in pretty good standing, but as the delivery day drew near for his new baby, he decided to call it quits for a while. He knew his place was by Peggy's side.

The baby boy was born on August 20, 1972. Chris's first look at the minutes-old infant was through a glass window at the hospital in Casper.

Anyone familiar with newborn babies knows that when children are born, their heads are all shriveled up and their color is a pale blue. As their circulation gets going, their color turns soft pink and their "prune-faces" start to take on a more normal appearance. An old rodeo cowboy, however, would have no way of knowing these things. As Chris gazed on the ugly baby through the window, he was convinced they had had a freak. He tried to hide his disappointment, and he smiled at Peggy and told her he would be back during visiting hours. He climbed into Rodeo Rose and pointed the truck into the hills. Popping the top on an old, hot beer which had been rolling around under the seat for a few weeks, he tried to collect his thoughts.

Up in the mountains, Chris got out of the vehicle and sat down on a stump in the shade of the pines. He gazed skyward and began thinking aloud.

"Ya know, God," he said, still looking at the clouds, "that sure is one ugly kid. But he's ours, and I'll raise him . . . I'll love him, you know, even if he *is* ugly."

By the time he got back to the hospital, the baby had changed considerably; his color was normal, the swelling had left his eyes, and his skin had settled into a more natural placement around his face. In fact, by this time, he was a very pretty baby. Chris was elated—his prayers had been answered.

The only bad thing about becoming a new father was Chris failed to qualify for the 1972 National Finals Rodeo because he had taken so much time off. It didn't really bother him, though; there was always next year. He had never been an impatient sort of person.

Chris had decided it was time to buy some land and settle down. He picked up a double lot outside of Kaycee with a small trailer house on it and began building a log cabin. The logs were cut from the Big Horn mountain and the flagstone was brought from the Blue Creek Ranch. It was an all-consuming task, but Chris was thrilled at his achievments. Soon, however, the snow began to fly, and it was time to call off the building for the winter.

Since he couldn't build, Chris began trapping and hunting. He had seen a movie about Jeremiah Johnson and fancied himself the finest kind of mountain man.

It was time to collect himself and his thoughts, to establish a place for his family, and to get right with himself. He spent time doing things that pleased him and things that pleased Peggy, and let rodeo slip by the wayside. It was a cleansing period. By staying away from rodeos for a couple of months, his body healed completely. And a powerful craving built up within him which would finally win him over and force him to aim Rodeo Rose back out onto the pavement once again.

This time, however, there was a box of diapers and a few extra blankets in the back of the car. During his brief hiatus, Chris had realized the most important thing in his life was his family. Rodeo, which had always been his first priority, was now in second place, with music third. So it never even occurred to them that Peggy and their young son, Clay, might stay home. From time to time, when there were too many rodeos scheduled too closely together and the distance between them too far apart to drive, Chris would leave them behind for a day or two. Then Peggy would set up camp at a big rodeo, such as Houston, while he flew to a couple of others and back again.

Occasionally they would take a week or two off and stay in Kaycee, but for the most part they were going down the road pretty hard. Everyone got used to seeing Chris, Peggy and young Clay. They had made up little cowboy booties, a hat and chaps for Clay, and even had tiny spurs for him. Chris beamed with pride as he showed him off to all of his rodeo "family."

By the time the 1973 National Finals Rodeo rolled around, Chris was standing tenth in the overall average in the bareback riding, guaranteeing him a berth. It was to be Peggy's first Finals, and Chris's first with the family.

They decided to go first-class and got a motel room. While Chris was getting sweaty and nervous about the go-arounds, Peggy had him out and about in Oklahoma City going Christmas shopping. It was very strange for Chris, who was accustomed to living and breathing rodeo during the NFR, to be out carrying packages and taking care of a baby.

He did fairly well in the first go-around, placing fifth with a score of seventy-four; but he bucked off in the second round, dashing his hopes of winning the Finals Buckle. He didn't let it discourage him, however, as he had learned long ago to take each go-around separately. He rode the rest of his horses out, and even split second/third place money in the fifth go-around with Sandy Kirby, who ended up winning the average that year.

Chris placed sixth in the average for the Finals and ended up in eleventh place in the overall standings. It had turned out to be a pretty fair year for him, but he was still craving that big gold buckle.

The biggest lesson Chris learned from his winter forays into the mountain wilderness in search of game was patience.

He had always known the value Indians placed on patience and calm endurance. By setting the right traps and then waiting for them to attract game, a hunter could emerge victorious in a contest involving life and death during a cold winter. By moving too soon, he could startle the intended game and lose out on a badly needed meal.

Chris cultivated his patience and endurance, and applied it to more than just hunting and trapping; it became a part of his very personality. He didn't need to "have it right now," as many people do; he was content to figure out a way to get whatever it was he wanted and then follow his plan, step by step, until he achieved his goal.

The cabin became a monument to his patience . . . and a joke to everyone else. When it was nice enough to work on the structure, he was off rodeoing, and when he wasn't on the rodeo trail, the weather was too cold for building. It took years to complete, but the cabin is standing to this very day.

Chris also used this patience in his quest for the World Championship. The time would come when, instead of missing his mark on the last horse, he would spur it out and win the Buckle. He also knew that he gained experience with time. His consistency was improving considerably, and he was learning how to get more points out of bad draws. It all amounted to more money in the pocket and a better outlook on the sport.

The only thing a rider could not depend on was his health. Chris knew he had been pretty lucky up to this point not to have had any serious injuries. If he could keep from getting busted up, he could keep going down the road for many more years; but one bad wreck and it could all be over in a heartbeat.

Like all professional athletes, rodeo cowboys are conditioned and trained, so the odds of serious injury are reduced to a minimum. But they still exist, and at almost every rodeo someone gets hurt pretty badly. Normally, a few stiches and some iodine and he's back up on another head in a few days. Occasionally, though, a rider will become seriously injured or crippled, and never be able to compete again. Sometimes a rider will wear his spurs into heaven. It's all part of the game, and every rodeo cowboy accepts the odds and does his best to stay off of the list of statistics.

Chris played the odds to his advantage in most cases, and hoped they would continue to fall on his side of the fence for a few more years—at least until he was able to win that elusive Gold Buckle.

Chapter 13

Photo Finish

At seven this morning I got on the phone
And said to hold my bronc as long as you can.
My car broke down in Billings, and I just got it put together,
I'll be photo finishing into old Cheyenne.

Well here I am in Sheridan and it's nine o'clock
In the morning, and time's a-goin' fast.
I just pulled her over, had some coffee and a doughnut,
And I bought the car a brand new tank of gas.

Well I don't know if I'm gonna make it,
It's nine fifteen; I'll be lucky if I ever get there.
By God, now what's that I hear? Is it a si-reen?
Sure enough, he got me on his radar.

He pulled up behind me and turned on those flashing lights,
A sign that I knew meant, "pull her over."
So I stomped on my brakes, and as I skidded to a halt,
I wiped out three reflector posts along the shoulder.

He got out of his car and was a-walkin' real slow,
So I jumped out and met him halfway.
He jerked out his gun and said, "Mister, are you crazy?
I ain't never seen nobody drive that way."

I told him to take it easy, and he could put up that cannon,
The way he's shakin, it just might go off.
He put up the gun, as I explained my situation,
He listened to my story, then he coughed.

He wrote me out a ticket that seemed to take forever,
I took it and headed for my car.
That cop, he hollered out to me and said, "Hey, cowboy,
You'd better slow down, 'cause you can't outrun this radar."

As I rolled down the road, I was a-cursin' and a-swearin'
About that ticket that I had just acquired,
I wondered if I should pay it, or throw it out the window.
Lit a match and set the damn thing fire.

So I gunned it once again, and was a travelin' down the road
With the gas pedal mashed to the floor,
When I came around a curve, and right there in the highway
There's more darned sheep than I've ever seen before.

I'm going too fast to ever stop, so I just closed my eyes
As the car roars on through the herd.
When I open up my eyes again, there's a sheep on the fender,
And that herder's sayin' some mighty awful words.

Sixty-fifty-forty-thirty-twenty miles more,
The rodeo starts in another eighteen minutes.
As I pull in through the main gate, and I hear the Anthem
* playing,*
I can't believe it—thank God I finally made it.

There's only one more obstacle that's standing in my way,
It's a nitwit with a weekend badge.
He's standing by the gate, and as I slide her to a halt,
He says, "Where in the hell you goin' so doggone fast?"

I tell him that I'm entered, and I ain't got time to talk,
My horse is in the chute and I'm late.
He says I need to get a pass from the secretary,
My eyes get red, my heart fills up with hate.

I yell, "You dirty so-and-so, you'd better let me through."
He asked if I'd repeat that once again,
So I whacked him in the mouth and left him lyin' there
On his back, a-kickin' in the sand.

I got there just in time to see my bronc come running out,
His head and tail was held way up high.
I swear he looked right straight at me, grinned and gave a horse
*   laugh,*
And me—I just stood there and cried.

I turned around feeling helpless and purely dumbfounded,
I looked, and what did I see?
Three highway patrolmen, and a gateman with a fat lip,
And they were all lookin' right at me.

Sittin' in this cell now, I've done a lot of thinking
About that wild run that I made a month ago.
I'm sorry that I'm in this rotten situation;
If I could do it again, I wouldn't have drove so slow!

Chris LeDoux (Wyoming Brand Music),
from **Rodeo Songs Old and New**

"Chicken one day and feathers the next," was the phrase Chris used most often to describe his life on the rodeo trail. If he was winning and had lots of money in his pocket, he and the family would stay in motels and eat in restaurants, he'd upgrade equipment and get Rosie worked on. But when he went into a slump, it was sleeping in the truck and campfires on the side of the road.

The young LeDouxs had a good year in 1974, as Chris's riding became more consistent. He won Baton Rouge and placed well at Houston and Ft. Worth; it seemed the more he won, the more confidence he built up within himself. As in previous years, Peggy and Clay still came to most of the shows, but there were always those isolated weeks when Chris would have to leave them behind to hit a bunch of rodeos in a short period of time.

The Calgary Stampede was a high point in any rodeo cowboy's season, and no less so for Chris. Since it was held at the same time as Sheridan, Wyoming, Chris would usually go up to Calgary alone and join up with Peggy and Clay back in Sheridan.

In 1974 Chris had arranged to charter an airplane out of Billings with a couple of other cowboys. The pilot would meet them in Calgary, after the short-go, then fly them back to Sheridan for the night performance, stopping at the border for customs. The customs stop is routine and usually only takes a few minutes.

Chris had drawn a horse called Necklace, out of Harry Vold's string, which had been voted Bareback Horse of the Year four separate times. He had seen the horse buck many times and had always yearned for the opportunity to ride her; now he had that chance.

Even before the performance started, the horse seemed to be aware of the swelling crowd and the mounting excitement in the air. First standing quietly in the chute, she began to pace nervously, then to kick and rear as it got closer to showtime.

"It's like she's one of us," Chris said to another bareback rider as they both watched the champion horse. He slipped his rigging on the brute and made ready for the gate. Knowing the caliber of the horse beneath him, he concentrated on making a power-ride. He knew he would have to get lots of drag with the spurs and muscle it out with the horse.

"They're gonna have to use dynamite to get me off of this horse," he thought as he ran his hand into the rigging handle.

Suddenly, his chute was surrounded by people: the usual crowd of flank men, gate men, and chute help—but also a bevy of photographers and cameramen. He had almost forgotten this was the world famous Calgary Stampede Rodeo; there was just barely enough room for him and Necklace in all of that crowd. He knew one sure way to put the crowd behind him, though, so he pulled his hat down tight and nodded his head. The gate cracked open, and Necklace exploded into the arena.

The horse had a habit of ducking and swooping during a ride, showing her belly to the crowd by rolling from side to side. An inexperienced rider usually ends up getting snapped from side to side, then flung over the front. Chris knew the secret to riding Necklace was in keeping the spurs firmly in her neck and getting lots of drag. The horse put on one heck of a showing, circling to the left and never missing a trick in her bid to launch the unwelcome passenger into the air.

The whistle sounded, and Chris pulled himself up with his free hand. When the judges tallied up the score, he had won the final go-around. Heaving a sigh of relief, he respectfully watched the great bucking horse trot out of the arena with her head and tail held proudly in the air.

Since one of the cowboys flying back to Sheridan was a calf roper, they all had to wait for that event to end before catching the plane. Then, on the way back into the U.S.A., they stopped at customs.

The small airstrip at which they had landed was located at an automobile-border crossing point, and there were only two inspectors for both the cars and the occasional airplane. After they taxied into position and shut down the engines, they could see a wildly painted van in an advanced state of disassembly at the roadside.

They got out of the airplane and walked over to the van. An inspector was inside with a set of tools, removing side panels. The seats had already been taken apart, the carpeting ripped out, and the headliner stripped down to the metal. Seeing the group of cowboys standing outside watching him, the customs agent paused a moment.

"What can I do for you boys?" he asked, looking them over.

"Just flew in from Calgary," answered the pilot. "We need to get cleared on to Sheridan. These boys are riding in a rodeo down there tonight."

The agent gave them a pained look. "Sorry boys, but it's going to be a little while. We found some dope in this van and have the occupants in a holding cell. The authorities are going to be here soon to pick them up, and I have to have this vehicle completely searched by then. You'll just have to wait until I'm done. I'll do the best I can.''

The cowboys walked back to the airplane and spent the next two hours nervously pacing about the airstrip, checking their watches. They were getting critically close to the wire on their timing if they were to make Sheridan in time for the barebacks. When they finally saw the van owners being loaded into the paddy wagon and the customs agent walking their way, Chris ran over to the pay telephone and called Peggy.

"Meet us at the airport," he told her, "and tell them to hold my horse as long as they can."

In a few minutes they were back in the air. The inspector apologized for the delay, and the boys all said they understood, but it didn't change the fact the rodeo wasn't going to wait.

"Hippies," one of them muttered in disgust.

When the plane landed on the small airstrip in Sheridan, Peggy was already in the tie-down area. She pulled up next to the plane in the International pickup truck she had borrowed from her father and waited for them with the engine still running. Quickly they tossed their gear down and loaded it into the back of the truck. The pilot climbed in next to Peggy, leaving Chris the outside, where he would have just a bit more room to get himself taped up. The calf roper, a cowboy named Bucky Bradford, scrambled into the back and held onto the "headache rack." Peggy had the gas pedal mashed to the floor even before the door was fully closed.

She powered out onto the main road leading to Sheridan, throwing gravel and dirt as they lurched onto the blacktop. To get to the rodeo grounds, they would have to drive through downtown Sheridan, then out of town on the far side.

Peggy knew the back roads fairly well and tried to avoid the tourist-crowded main thoroughfares. However, in changing lanes too quickly on an unavoidable thoroughfare, she sideswiped a car with New York plates. Peggy began to stop the truck, but Chris told her to keep going, and Bucky hollered to the driver of the car to just follow them to the rodeo and they'd work out the damages later.

The New Yorker was too confused to say anything, so he just nodded his head and followed Peggy. She jammed the gas pedal back down to the floor; the New Yorker followed suit, and Peggy could see the little man driving the car in her rearview mirror, grinning from ear to ear, apparently enjoying the whirlwind tour of Sheridan.

In the cab of the truck, Chris was carefully wrapping tape around his riding arm and getting spurred-up. There would be very little, if any, time at the grounds for preparations. He looked at his watch ... they had just seven minutes to go until the rodeo started.

They left the main road and motored up the small dirt track which lead to the back gate. Chris could see a stocky man in a uniform walking out into the middle of the road.

"Aw, shoot," Chris said, seeing the small badge on the big man's chest. "It's a weekend supercop. Peg, you just drive when I tell you to drive, you hear?"

She nodded her understanding as she slammed on the brakes, coming to a stop just inches away from the gate guard, who had put his hands down on the hood of the truck like Superman, trying to stop the vehicle. Chris immediately leaned out of the window and began hollering at the man to get out of the way. He told the guard that his horse was already in the chute—they could hear the National Anthem playing—and they didn't have time to play games.

The man hollered back that nobody was going to crash *his* gate, and if they wanted in they'd have to get passes. The New Yorker, meanwhile, had pulled up behind them and was standing outside his car, watching the exchange from a safe distance.

Chris and the gateman had a few more words, then the big man lost his temper. He rushed around to the side of the truck and jerked Chris's door open. Chris, not much of a fighter, had learned long ago the best thing a smaller guy can do is get in the first punch, then keep punching as hard and as fast as he can. When the car door was jerked open, Chris popped out like a jack-in-the-box and slammed his fist into the jaw of the bigger man. The guard went down, with Chris on top of him.

In all of the excitement, Peggy allowed the car to roll forward a few feet; in the process, she ran up onto Chris's boot, pinning him to the ground. He commenced pounding on the big man as he hollered for Peggy to get off of his foot. She didn't understand him at first but finally rolled forward. Chris jumped up, with the gateman grasping at him, and ran for the gate.

"Drive, drive!" he yelled.

She stepped on the gas, and Chris ran as fast as he could behind her. The New York tourist didn't miss a lick and spun right into the dust cloud left swirling behind the truck. He was having the time of his life.

Just as the truck crossed the track which surrounds the arena, Chris caught up and dove into the back. Looking around, he noticed a couple of other guards listening intently to their radios. He knew the man at the back gate was blowing the whistle on him.

Chris grabbed his rigging bag, and as Peggy pulled up to the fence behind the chutes, he popped out of the truck and tossed his bag over. Just as it hit the ground, a cowboy was being thrown through the air by a wild bucking horse inside the arena. Chris looked at the animal and recognized it as his own draw. When he hadn't shown up on time, the contractor had given it to an un-entered cowboy for an exhibition ride, rather than turn the horse into the arena.

"Oh no," Chris said aloud, gazing at his horse. Slowly backing down from the fence, he turned to see the gateman, with a radio held up to his bleeding mouth, running toward him. Off to the left he could see two other uniformed guards, and behind the truck, the New Yorker was getting out to look at the damage to his car from the accident in Sheridan. Chris gulped, "Man, this just don't look like it's gonna be my day," he said to himself.

As it turned out, Chris got off with an apology to the gate man, and the New Yorker had had so much fun getting a first-hand look at those "wild and rowdy cowboys," he told Chris to just forget about the damage to his car.

Later that month, Chris drew up well at Cheyenne, a rodeo that had always been dear to his heart. He still had visions of his boyhood, when he had performed for the prairie dogs on his old buckskin, Comanche. He scored an arena record (which was to last a full twenty-four hours) of eighty-six points on Cervi's Dark Canyon to easily win the first go-around.

He placed in the second go-around and went into the short-go with a ten-point lead over second-place Joe Alexander, at that time the reigning World Champion and a three-time winner. Chris had drawn a buckskin horse named Tightrope for the round, and he knew it would be an honest ride.

He rode the horse well and scored an incredible eighty-two points—the trophy buckle was as good as his. But he hadn't counted on the performance about to be turned in by Joe Alexander.

Joe had drawn a horse named Marlboro, and he knew he needed to make one heck of a ride to beat Chris. He decided to just lay back and give it everything he had. The horse responded by exploding powerfully out of the chute, turning back in a circle to the right, with Joe screwed down tight for the ride. When the dust finally settled, the judges awarded him ninety-three record-setting points for his effort—and he beat Chris out by a single point in the average.

By winning a go-around and taking second in the average, Chris did make out fairly well financially, but he would never again come so close to winning Old Cheyenne.

In September, Chris realized that, while he was doing extremely well, he had no hope of catching Joe Alexander in the overall year-end standings, but he was high enough in the standings that he could afford to take a couple of months off the rodeo circuit and still qualify for the Finals. So he decided to work on his cabin and spend more time with the family in Kaycee. In November, he went back out to a few rodeos to get sharpened up for the NFR, and in December he went into Oklahoma City in the number-three spot in the overall standings.

Joe Alexander was over ten thousand dollars out in front of Chris and the number-two rider, Rusty Riddle. Rusty had a good NFR and caught up a few points on Joe, but, like Chris, had no serious hope of winning the year-end award. Rusty finished third in the average.

Chris won the tenth go-around but had two no-scores in previous rounds that pretty well counted him out of the money in the average. Jack Ward, a good friend of Chris's from Odessa, Texas, won the Finals Buckle that year, with Larry Mahan taking second in the average. T.J. Walter finished with one of his better years and had enough left over for a fifth place showing in the average.

His patience still not worn thin, Chris felt that 1975 would be as good a year as any for him to capture the title. He went back to Kaycee feeling good about himself and renewing his resolve to win the World.

Chapter 14

He's a Tryer

He's a rider, keeps ridin' all he can 'cause he's a tryer,
Keeps tryin' all he can, 'cause he never seems to know he's
* had enough.*
And it gets rough.
He's been boozin'. He ain't a drunk, he's just forgettin' that
* he's losin'.*
Forgettin' pain his mind and body feels, and he needs a meal.

He's a cowboy. He's country bred and strong, yeah, he's a
* cowboy.*
And he'd rather take the pain than face the shame and face
* the judge down deep inside.*
Well it's just pride.
So he'll keep goin', keep tryin' hard to ride instead of throwin'
'Cause he just won't admit he's growing old.
The thought's too cold.

He'll keep tryin', 'cause he still recalls the days when it paid off,
When he was winning; you can bet he won a lot more than
* he lost.*
He ain't no quitter, no one can talk him out of movin' on,
'Cause he's a tryer, and he's damn sure, his second chance'll
* come before too long.*

Billy Bob Shane (Wyoming Brand Music),
from **Used To Want To Be a Cowboy**

Early in February 1975, the odds finally caught up with Chris.
He had drawn a little horse named Cripple Creek at the Hous-

ton rodeo. The horse just scattered and didn't buck worth a darn, but Chris gave it his all. When the whistle sounded, the pick-up men moved to get Chris off the animal's back, and one of them tried to cut off the racing horse.

Cripple Creek tried to duck behind the pick-up horse but didn't quite make it. He ran into the other animal's hind-quarter, spun slightly sideways, stumbled and went down. Chris's hand was still bound in the rigging handle, and when Cripple Creek went down, he tried to roll with the animal, but his left leg got pinned under the brute and he heard it snap as he pulled his hand free from the handle. The horse struggled back to his feet and dashed off, but Chris lay still.

He had torn all of the ligaments loose in his left knee, although he didn't know it at the time. Both legs were completely numb, but Chris tried to get up anyway. A couple of cowboys quickly dashed to his side and helped him out of the arena.

Out in the back of the chutes, Chris sat down and waited for the pain and numbness to subside. He was finally able to stand up and could begin to assess the damage. A burning pain was in his left knee, reminding him of an injury he had received years ago playing football. That time, he had torn some cartilage in the knee and it had healed on its own, with a fair amount of time off.

Diagnosing this injury as the same, Chris decided he'd probably be better in a week or so and feel well enough to ride at San Angelo, Texas, the next weekend—with a little luck and a lot of tape. He and Peggy loaded up Rosie and headed for their little trailer so Chris could take the weight off his knee and start the recuperation process.

The next morning Chris received a visit from his brother Mike, who was in Houston selling records and tapes in a booth at the rodeo. Mike grew concerned about his knee when Chris told him he'd barely been able to get out of bed that morning because of the pain. Chris asked Mike if he would drive down to a pharmacy and buy him a pair of crutches. Mike agreed, and soon Chris was hobbling about on the implements.

Chris and Peggy stayed in Houston to watch the rest of the rodeo, then they hooked up the trailer and pointed Rosie toward San Angelo.

Chris went to the college at San Angelo and was allowed to use the whirlpool a few times. However, the day before he was scheduled to ride, there was no significant improvement in the leg, and he arrived at the bitter conclusion he would have to turn out his horse and take a couple of weeks off. They loaded up Rosie and headed back north to Wyoming.

The "couple of weeks" he had intended to lay off stretched out into nearly two months, as the knee was damaged pretty badly. The ache subsided to the point where he could walk around a bit, but any sudden movement caused a bolt of pain to shoot through the knee. He began experimenting with various ways to tape it up, thus reducing the possibility of re-injury during the healing process.

In April, he packed up Peggy, Clay and their camping trailer and headed out to Nashville. Al had invited them out for a visit, and since his rodeoing was temporarily on hold, he accepted. It would also give Chris a chance to cut another rodeo album.

Al had long ago noticed Chris's musical talents and had encouraged him often in his younger years. After the time Chris tried unsuccessfully to peddle his songs on Music Row, Al and Bonnie worked out a strategy for developing and marketing some of Chris's music on their own—as a family business.

Chris's first foray into the Nashville recording studios was during the break between the 1971 NFR and his wedding to Peggy a few weeks later. He put "Mountain Wild Man," "Riverboat Gambler," "Colorado," and "Ain't No Place for a Country Boy" on tape, as well as a few other songs that he'd written.

The original tape was tediously copied at home, with Bonnie, Al and Chris's sister Jeannie and brother Mike pitching in to help. They slowly churned out hundreds of copies, and in the process American Cowboy Songs, Inc., was created.

Chris filled his rigging bag with the tapes and began selling them as he went "down the road," to supplement his rodeo earnings.

Sales were slow at first but rapidly grew, and the demand for more tapes and new songs saw Chris return to Nashville several more times in the ensuing years. The record company showed a steady and consistent profit and ultimately grew to include other artists performing cowboy music.

A few weeks after the record had been cut, Chris was getting rodeo fever again and decided to try out his leg. He entered a rodeo in Shelbyville, Tennessee, and soon the family was on its way. Chris had drawn a little yellow horse and, prior to the ride, had carefully taped and wrapped the left knee. When he nodded his head, the horse turned out into the arena, and Chris laid back and put the spurs to him. For the first four or five seconds, things really felt good, but then the horse ducked back just enough for Chris to get a solid hold with the left spur. Instantly, the knee pulled apart again, and the pain all but immobilized him. He double-grabbed and pulled himself up; his left leg hung uselessly. The pick-up man snatched him off and carried him gently to the side of the arena, where he could use the fence to support himself.

He knew all of his plans for "going hard" in 1975 would have to wait. This injury was a lot more serious than Chris had figured. They headed back to Kaycee, where Chris finally consulted a doctor.

The ligaments were severely torn and he was told they needed to be surgically repaired. Chris didn't want to go through with that, nor was he sure it was just the right thing to do. He also didn't like the idea of being laid up for so long after surgery. So he decided to do it *his* way—let nature work on the injury.

He also worked on new and more creative methods to tape the knee to significantly reduce stress placed on the joint during a ride. After a few months, he felt he had made some pretty good progress and couldn't wait to try it out.

In late June Chris entered North Platte, Nebraska, and drew a horse named Mountain Belle. The tape-job seemed to work, and Chris placed well enough on the horse to make the short go-around.

In the short go, he had drawn a horse named Top Out. This time, the horse turned back hard, and Chris had to dig in with his spurs for a good grip, causing the knee to pop out of place again.

It was back to the drawing board. In addition to waiting a little, taping well, and trying to ease up on the left leg in the spur-ride, he knew he would have to do something else. After careful thought, he figured a shorter shank on his spurs would help reduce the amount of drag.

He had Bob Blackwood make him up a pair of one-and-three-quarter-inch shank spurs, and a few weeks later he cracked out again. This time it was a little better, although he never felt really comfortable. Needless to say, he spent a lot of time in Kaycee, very little on the rodeo trail, and was well out of the qualifications for the NFR in December.

He was invited to Oklahoma City anyway to perform some of his music, which had started to gain in popularity. The small "riggin' bag business" was starting to grow into a fairly lucrative enterprise, with Al basically running the show from Nashville.

By this time Chris had cut five albums: *Songs of Rodeo Life, Rodeo Songs Old and New, Songs of Rodeo and Country, Rodeo and Living Free,* and the one they had recorded earlier that year, *Life as a Rodeo Man.* The music gave Chris an opportunity to make a little extra money while his injuries healed. It was still not a driving force in his life—although, he had to admit, he had never been bucked off a guitar. His albums were in demand everywhere he went, but he really had no desire to quit rodeoing and go down the concert trail in its stead.

Being in Oklahoma City as a non-contestant may have been good for his music career, but it was a godsend for his rodeo career. To be so close to the action and not be a part of it was almost too much for him. He played his music and watched the go-arounds, and with each passing day, he became more maniacal in his disposition. He really wanted to get on those ponies. Finally, when he thought he could take no more, it was over, and he was able to pack up Rodeo Rose and head home.

With his resolve renewed by the NFR, Chris established a very rigid training program designed to strengthen his knee and to put him back in peak competitive form. His regimen included a special diet, a daily run, both long distance runs and sprints, basketball, hay-bale kicking, and working out on a bucking machine he had borrowed. Each day, as he mounted the machine or the hay bale, he would picture Necklace, Smokey, Spark Plug, Three Bars, Moonshine, or High Tide, all Bareback Horses of the Year at one time or another since Chris had begun rodeoing. He could smell the rosin and feel the bolting, snorting stock in the chute beneath him. A thousand times he spurred the beast to victory, and a thousand times he climbed off to find he was still in Kaycee.

Finally Denver rolled around, and Chris was off to a real rodeo with a real horse. Peggy and Clay came along, because now that they had the small camping trailer to tote along behind Rosie, they always had "home" with them, wherever they parked.

At Denver, Chris rode fairly well; but most importantly, he rode comfortably. His body was holding together, and the training was beginning to pay off.

After Denver they hit Ft. Worth and San Antonio, then down to Houston for the same rodeo at which he had been hurt the previous year. He came back strong, and for the first time in his career, he won the average there.

Chris steadily rose up in the standings, finding himself in fourth place overall in the RCA when he drove down to Phoenix. He had drawn a horse named Molly Brown, on which Jack Ward had ridden earlier. Jack was currently standing in first place for his ride on the horse.

"She's a little bit pregnant," Jack explained to Chris, who listened closely, "so you really have to cinch 'er down tight to keep that riggin' from slipping over her head." And she realy fired hard out there.

"Shoot," replied Chris, "she's always been just a little strong, anyway, hasn't she?"

"She still is," answered Jack positively, rubbing his riding arm.

Chris made ready for the ride and lowered himself down into the chute. He had pulled the latigos so tightly the rigging body didn't move an inch. Then he ran his hand in and nodded his head. Molly Brown turned into the arena with a powerful surge that threw Chris all the way back to the end of his arm.

Within a few jumps, he was setting into a pretty good spur-lick, but he could tell she was really taking everything he had, especially on his riding arm, and she wasn't giving any change. It was a terrible jerking around for LeDoux, but considering the horse under him, he was doing magnificently.

Suddenly, Chris felt a small snap in his left shoulder, and a tingle ran up his arm. For just a second, he didn't think much of it—then, as Molly lunged forward in a high-dive again, he reached the end of his arm and it came alive in pain. In two more jumps he was forced to double grab and pull up as the punishment became unbearable. It felt as if someone were hitting him on the shoulder with a sledgehammer.

Chris went to see a doctor, having learned his lesson the previous year about waiting, and found he had pulled his collarbone loose. Each time the horse had jumped, the severed end of the bone stabbed him in the neck. The doctor put him in a brace, gave him some pain pills, and sent him on his way back to Kaycee.

Chris spent the remainder of the spring around the house, working on the log cabin and taking care of their little place. After the initial shock of the injury wore off, he found he could do almost anything he wanted without pain—except ride horses.

It proved a blessing to his cabin project, as he finally had the time and the right weather to place the stones in the fireplace, run wiring, and the rest. He also worked on ways to tape the shoulder so it wouldn't hurt so badly and continued to work out, trying not lose his edge.

After a few months off the circuit, he finally entered Kileen, Texas, and Tulsa, Oklahoma. To keep the expenses down, Chris left the family at home and hitched rides with a few other cowboys.

He drew a nice little horse in Kileen which just jumped and kicked, bucking like a rocking chair, and didn't cause him too much pain or discomfort. He wore a shoulder harness and applied yards of tape to his knee, as well as the usual wrist and arm taping. He had to make sure there would be no more "photo finishes" in his career, since it now took him nearly an hour just to get taped and strapped up for a ride.

His confidence had been bolstered by the ride in Kileen, but he also knew the horse had played a key part in his success; it had bucked off to the right, putting the least amount of strain on the arm, with no ducking or diving to put pressure on the shoulder.

In Tulsa, however, Chris drew the 1972 Bareback Horse of the Year, from Harry Void's string, called Smokey. Chris knew Smokey wasn't going to cooperate in any way, shape, form or fashion. Smokey would put everything he had into the contest with the rider, and as strong as he was, he had a lot. Chris knew he was not physically up to that kind of punishment and decided to turn Smokey out. It was a decision he hated to make, knowing how tough a competitor the horse was.

However, since Tulsa was "on the way home," he decided to stop by and watch the action. But a few hours before the rodeo, Chris changed his mind and decided to ride. Soon, he was back behind the chutes putting on his sling and wrapping the yards of tape around his body he hoped would hold him together. He just couldn't pass up an opportunity to ride a bronc like Smokey, and his craving got the better of his senses.

From the first jump, Chris knew he'd bitten off more than he could chew. The sheer strength of the horse was a match for Molly Brown, the horse that had originally caused the damage to a perfectly healthy shoulder, and Smokey was applying the same kind of punishment to a frail shoulder. Chris pulled hard with his feet, trying to absorb as much of the shock as he could with his legs, but when Smokey turned back to the left, extending the riding arm, everything fell apart. He knew from that first twinge in his collar that to continue would be sheer folly. He double-grabbed and ended the ride before the whistle.

Back in Kaycee, the doctor told Chris there was nothing they could do to expedite the healing process; he should just keep it immobile and take it easy. That wasn't good enough for Chris; he had to do something *now*. He contacted a professional trainer for advice on how to tape the shoulder and was soon getting a lesson in anatomy. He learned how the different pieces of the shoulder fit together, and how they could be taped to move stress away from a weak joint and spread it among the healthier joints and bones.

Of course, he still had to take some time off to heal enough even to try the new taping technique, since he was basically in the same condition after Tulsa as he had been after Phoenix. But now he knew what he had to do when he was feeling almost normal again to avoid re-injuring himself.

He spent hours painfully working the muscles and ligaments back into condition, taking it one day at a time. He continued to work out on the track, running a mile or two, then finishing with sprints. The knee hadn't been too much trouble, but he intended to keep it that way. In July, he assessed himself as ready to get back on another head of roughstock.

In the latter part of 1975, the Association changed its rules governing the crowning of the World Champion and the awarding of the big Gold Buckle. Up to this point, the World Title was won by the biggest money-winner in each event at year's end, including the NFR, regardless of who won the

Finals. The Finals average winner won a nice silver buckle, but not the World's Champion Buckle Chris had always dreamed of earning.

In 1976, however, all of this changed. The person who won the most money at the NFR, regardless of money won prior to the Finals, would be proclaimed "World's Champion" and awarded the Gold Buckle. For this reason, Chris decided that this year, of all years, he would have to qualify for the Finals, no matter what else happened. (In 1979 the PRCA elected to return to the old way of selecting World Champions.) The race to earn the most money wasn't nearly as important as in previous years, since the man who went to the Finals in the fifteenth hole had as good a chance to win the Gold Buckle as the first-place man.

When Chris decided to try out his new taping technique in July, he was still in the top fifteen, but slipping quickly from his lack of recent winnings. He knew he would have to make some more money soon or slip from the list of qualifiers for the NFR. He also knew that, if this new technique didn't work and he re-injured the arm, he would be out for another two months or more and well out of the running. By the time he would be able to compete, most likely he would not be able to win enough to make the list again. It was now or never.

In Laramie, Wyoming, Chris applied tape to his shoulder, as he had been taught, and prayed for it to work. Even after the tape was on and his shirt was slipped over the job, he felt terribly uneasy about getting in the chute with his horse. He knew that, no matter what happened, it was going to hurt. In the very best instance, it would simply hurt less than the very worst instance. But either way, he'd be in pain, and that makes it hard to just walk up and jump on.

He lowered himself into the chute and nodded his head.

Miraculously, the shoulder held! Chris pulled himself up after the ride and could feel the pain throbbing through the shoulder as muscles and tendons protested their abuse, but the shoulder hadn't separated, and the collarbone had stayed in place. He cradled his sore arm across his belly and walked back to the chutes with a slight grin on his face.

He began entering rodeos again, always careful of the condition of his body, and soon was winning. All through July and August he rodeoed hard and was firmly established in the national bareback standings by the end of the Labor Day melee. He carefully calculated his overall position, and those beneath him on the list, and figured he'd surely be in the top fifteen, no matter what happened—so he went back home.

He worked on the cabin and allowed himself to heal. Meanwhile, he carefully watched the standings in each new issue of the *ProRodeo Sports News*, making sure his name was still on the list.

The last rodeo which counted toward qualification for the NFR was San Francisco, after which Chris was in fourteenth place in the PRCA. He had calculated it right down to the wire, but he had made it and was going to the National Finals Rodeo. Now all he had to do was win the most money in Oklahoma City and he would have that World's Champion Buckle he had always dreamed of owning. It was just ten short rides away—for the right cowboy.

Chapter 15

It Ain't the Years, It's the Miles

I walked behind the chute, strapped my spurs to my boots,
At that big rodeo in Cheyenne,
Feelin' tired and sore from a ride the day before
And a thousand other rides since I began.
As I climbed up the gate, I heard that young cowboy say,
"Well, that old man ain't gonna ride,"
And I had to smile.

I said, "Son, it ain't age that makes me look this way—
It ain't the years, boy, it's the miles.
It ain't the years that I've known that have taken their toll,
They've been few.
If you took all the mashin's, the draggin's and the crashin's,
You'd prob'ly look the same way that I do.
It's a million miles of road, of getting snatched around and
  throwed,
That finally put the cramp in my style.
It ain't age that makes me look this way,
It ain't the years, boy, it's the miles."

Went on and made my ride, only scored a sixty-five,
But you know what really made my day complete?
Was when I looked up just in time to see that young cowboy
  go flying,
And land in a pile at my feet.
And as the First-Aid came to haul him away,
I said, "Son, you'll be alright in a little while."

He's on his way to finding out, what it's all about,
It ain't the years, boys, it's the miles.

Chris LeDoux (Wyoming Brand Music),
from **Thirty-Dollar Cowboy**

Most of October found Chris busily working on the log house or out hunting in the mountains. Either diversion provided a lot of time for Chris to think, and he thought mostly about bucking horses. He thought about past triumphs and tragedies, of winning rides and stupid mistakes. He thought about his body and began to realize his own vulnerability. While his patience was still holding strong, he knew his body would not continue to take the abuse he was forcing upon it. The end of his rodeo career became a very real inevitability for Chris. He knew if he was ever going to win the World, he'd better do it soon, before his body fell completely apart.

In early November Chris began making plans for a serious training regimen. He knew there were a lot of factors involved with the NFR that were beyond his control, such as the luck of the draw; but the one thing he had complete control over was his own physical fitness. He resolved to be in the very best condition he had ever been in in his entire life before the rodeo began.

He began daily exercises, as well as a lot of stretching. He also took to the high school track, pulling on his tennis shoes and an old sweatshirt, and ran.

Winter was fast closing its grip on Kaycee; the leaves were gone from the trees and the grass had already turned brown. The cold air burned Chris's tired lungs as he pushed himself nearly to exhaustion each day. But he could feel himself getting closer to winning the title, and it kept the desire burning within him to push ever harder. Always, whether running, playing basketball, doing push-ups, or just sitting around the house in the evenings, the visions of bucking horses dominated Chris's thoughts. Peggy understood that faraway look he would get in his eyes, when he had drifted into a rodeo arena in his mind.

Chris called a young cowboy friend of his, Lionel Ellison, who owned a bucking machine. He wanted to rent the machine, but Lionel's father picked up the phone and interrupted the conversation.

"No, you can't rent it," Mr. Ellison said, pretending to be angry. "But I'll be happy to bring it down to you, if you'll just promise to go to the Finals and beat 'em.'' He could almost hear the smile on the elder man's face as he concluded the statement. Chris was delighted.

The whole Ellison family came with Lionel and his father to wish Chris well and help set up the heavy bucking machine in Bud Rhoad's shop. When they were on their way again, Chris headed over to his house to get his rigging bag.

Back at the shop, with Peggy at his side, he gazed at the silent machine among the other tools and equipment in the room. Chris felt it would surely make all of the difference in the world in helping get him ready for the NFR.

Chris had learned years ago, while playing football in school, that you never play in a real game any better than you practice. If you practice at half speed all week, you'll play half speed in the game as well. Applying this idea to rodeo, Chris resolved to give it one hundred percent each and every time he climbed onto the bucking machine.

In preparation for his inaugural ride, he taped-up, spurred-up and stretched out, just as he would have done at a real rodeo. Then he began the mental preparations as well; in his mind, he was about to mount the toughest horse in the world, not a piece of cold steel and plastic. He strapped on his glove and climbed onto the machine. Peggy stood ready with the controls.

As he ran his hand into the rigging, in his mind he was straddling Necklace or Three-Bars, and his heart was racing in anticipation of the ride. He nodded his head, and the machine lurched to life. It had all the power of a strong horse and a lot of drop to the front end. Chris knew he would be tested to the limit. As it creaked and clanged, he concentrated as he had never done before on the mental picture of the horse beneath him.

"Get stronger," he told himself. "Pull your riggin'. Toes out, lots of drag." After about twelve seconds, he double-grabbed and Peggy shut it down. The silence was overpowering in the little shop.

Chris sat atop the bucking machine, his heaving breath coming in foggy blasts and his heart pounding in his chest so loudly he was certain even Peggy could hear it from where she stood. Slowly, he looked up.

"I've got a lot of work to do," he said quietly, "but I'll be ready." Peggy walked over to him and gave him a reassuring hug. She would be there beside him each and every day, working the controls and lending moral support.

A few weeks earlier they had learned Peggy was again pregnant and decided it would be better, for the baby's sake, if she and Clay were to stay home this year. Chris knew Peggy wanted to go to Oklahoma City almost as badly as he did, but they both realized that, no matter how important rodeo was, the family came first and foremost.

The days raced past, and Chris could feel himself getting stronger and more confident with each trip on the bucking machine. When it was time to pack up and get ready to leave, Peggy and Clay followed him out to the truck, and he kissed each of them good-bye. Reluctantly, Chris climbed into Rodeo Rose and pulled out on the highway by himself.

Gathered in Oklahoma City to decide the World Championship in the bareback riding event were Joe Alexander, Jimmy Dix, Royce Smith, T.J. Walter, Bruce Ford, Rusty Riddle, Sandy Kirby, Ike Sankey, J.C. Trujillo, Jack Ward, Sam Perkins, Glen Ford, Chick Elms, Mickey Young—and Chris.

Chris knew that, although he had been to several NFR's before this, 1976 would probably be the most important NFR he had ever attended. He had a good shot at the World's Ti-

tle, since he was the healthiest he had been in two years, probably the best shape he had *ever* been in. He had also gained
valuable experience and stock knowledge over the past few
years which would help him prepare mentally for each ride.

After arriving in Oklahoma City, the contestants were invited to a Calcutta, an event wherein the contestants are auc-
tioned off to the highest bidders. The money all goes into a
jackpot, and the person who "buys" the contestant who
ultimately wins the event will win the jackpot. Like the rodeo
itself, bareback riding was the first event featured, and the
highest prices were commanded by champions Joe Alexander
and Jack Ward.

Chris was "bought" by Mel Potter for a bargain-basement
price, which should have hurt Chris's feelings, but due to his
record of injuries and low standing coming into the Finals,
he could understand. Instead, he felt Mel had purchased a
real bargain; only Chris could know the peak physical condition he was in.

As an NFR veteran, Chris felt the best policy was to take
it one horse at a time. For this reason, he didn't make it his
goal to win the average, or even the most money; his goal was
simply to ride each horse he drew, in each go-around, the very
best he could. He would let the rest take care of itself.

After the Calcutta was over, the cowboys headed back to
the Holiday Inn, where the draw would be posted each night
for the next day's performance. Chris recognized his draw,
out of the Cervi Rodeo string, called Devil's Dream, since she
had helped him win the Houston rodeo. She was a pretty little horse, but Chris knew he'd have his hands full. He went
up to his room and turned in.

He arrived at the coliseum a few hours before performance
time and could really feel the tension building. Chris was getting too tight for his own good, and he knew it. Then he heard
J.C. Trujillo let loose with a "Yee-ha!" behind the chutes.

Chris grinned. "Thank God for J.C.," he said to himself.
J.C. was always joking around behind the chutes and having
a good time. "He's right. This shouldn't be so darned serious.

It should be fun—even if it is the Finals." J.C.'s attitude seemed to rub off just a little on everyone, and soon they were all a bit more relaxed.

Chris spent quite some time getting taped up and ready for the ride. His knee came first, then his shoulder and arm. Those who saw him say he rivaled any wartime veteran for bandages. Many of the younger riders and rookies looked at him and had second thoughts about rodeo as a career. Others, of course, felt that *they* would never wind up so bandaged and bent, but of course only the miles would tell.

He lowered himself down onto Devil's Dream, nodded his head, and let it rip. He was thrilled to be back on a real horse again instead of the mechanical monstrosity he'd been riding for the past few weeks. The first part of the ride went very well, but then he spurred out over the neck, throwing himself just slightly out of balance. He recovered well, but the judges would mark him down some for the error. They ended up awarding him a score of sixty-four, which put him in eleventh place at the end of the first go-around. Greeley, Colorado, cowboy Bruce Ford had won the first go with a score of eighty-three, earned atop Walt Alsbaugh's Spark Plug, the 1974 Bareback Horse of the Year.

Always looking for the bright side to every situation, Chris wasn't the least bit disappointed by his showing. His body hadn't fallen apart, and he was still in the running for the average. Any score was better than a no-score, for Chris knew that one no-score would put that Gold Buckle out of reach for him this year.

In the the second go, Chris drew Cotton Rosser's good little yellow horse Grinnin' Bird and vowed to really bear down and try. He had talked to Royce Smith about the horse earlier, and Royce had said he was "just right—good to ride." When he nodded his head for the horse, T.J. Walter was leading the go-around with a score of seventy-six, turned in on Foxy, out of the Rafter H string. Chris got a smooth spur-lick in, and the judges awarded him a score of eighty, which was good enough for the win. Royce had been right!

Before each ride, and often during the day, Chris's thoughts would drift back to Wyoming, to Peggy and Clay, and while he did manage to keep his concentration up, he also felt lonely without "the crew." He called frequently, especially after winning nearly twelve hundred dollars in the second go-around.

Back in the dressing room before the third go-around, Chris was getting taped up and thinking again of his family. He thought about what he was doing in Oklahoma City, and it suddenly occurred to him what was most important. He looked up toward the heavens and said a quiet little prayer:

"Lord, I sure want to thank you for letting me make it to the Finals. I'm not going to ask you to help me win it, but I would like to ask you to help Peggy through this pregnancy, because that baby's more important than any gold buckle. Thank you, Lord. Amen."

Chris drew up a horse called Buster Brown, out of the Rafter-H string, for his third ride. He had seen the horse earlier in the year at a rodeo in Kansas, when his then traveling partner, T.R. Wilson, had him. The horse turned T.R. every way but loose, ducking and diving and rolling his belly to the sky. He was real strong, and Chris knew he'd have to ride him jump for jump and muscle it out with him.

True to form, the horse did his nastiest tricks, but Chris stayed with him. It's always difficult to get a good score on a horse like that because you can't get into a fluid spurring rhythm. A rider just gets his licks in when he can and hopes for the best. Chris ended up with a sixty-seven. Seven cowboys finished higher, with Rusty Riddle turning in an incredible ride on a horse called Strawberry, out of Sonny Linger's herd. Strawberry would go on to be voted the Bareback Horse of the Year in 1976. Rusty won the third round with a score of eighty-five.

Even though he hadn't won anything in the third go-around, Chris felt he had ridden Buster Brown as well as anyone could have. His confidence was building, and his body was staying strong. His shoulder and knee were feeling great, and he was in a good position in the average.

In the fourth go-around, Chris drew a runner named Poison Creek, out of Stephens herd, and the judges awarded him a re-ride. Chris hustled back behind the chutes and threw his rigging on the designated re-ride horse, Two Grand, belonging to Sutton. Chris knew this to be a fairly good mount, but for some reason, this time it too failed to buck.

Now totally out of breath, Chris was awarded a second re-ride and given a few minutes to recover. They ran his third horse in, Dark Moment, out of the Beutler Brothers & Cervi Rodeo Company. The horse was a little nervous in the chute, pacing about in the tight space. He was known to take a pretty good jump out of the chute, which sometimes made him hard to mark, but Chris was ready for him. His ride came during the saddlebronc competition, and he scored a seventy-five. It wasn't enough to win the go, but it did put him in third place. Mickey Young won the round on Red Dail, belonging to Stephens, with a score of eighty-one.

He couldn't wait to call Peggy with the news. Better than just winning third, he had also ridden three horses in less than an hour and held up. His doubts about being able to endure the Finals and all ten go-arounds were beginning to fade.

The day after the fourth go-around was a Monday, and everyone had the day off. The competitors were thankful for the respite, as most were beginning to feel pretty battered. J.C. Trujillo had a membership to a local health club, and he invited Chris to go with him to the facility. Chris eagerly agreed, and the nice steam bath, whirlpool and swim really helped his sore muscles.

On weekdays, Chris and several of the other cowboys would gather in Bruce and Glen Ford's motel room to pick a little guitar and discuss the bucking horses. They also talked about their injuries and offered advice on taping and riding techniques to reduce the severity of the wounds.

The fifth go-around saw Chris on a horse called Holy Smoke, from the Northcott Rodeo herd. It was an unusually cold night, and the wind was blowing up the alleyway into the building. From their warmup arena out back, Chris could see the horses' breath as they stood in the chutes. Holy Smoke was reputed to be a good, honest horse that would just jump and kick, without any fancy moves.

The National Finals Rodeo brings out the very best in both man and beast, it seems, for the very electricity in the air charges the two-legged and the four-legged performers equally. Holy Smoke, shedding its usually passive personality, fired into the arena, ducking left, then planting its feet and shooting straight up. The animal reared on its hind legs and whirled around, trying in vain to throw Chris to the dust. It was a spectacular display, but one which didn't really impress the judges; they awarded Chris a score of sixty-eight for his Herculean efforts.

The crowd hissed and booed the judges, and Chris felt a bit of disappointment but counted himself lucky for just having gotten past the volatile mount.

The fifth go-around would be recorded as "the great eliminator." The reigning World's Champion Joe Alexander was bucked off of Circle D's Knothead; J.C. Trujillio broke his hand on Cervi's St. Marie and was out for the rest of the week; Jimmy Dix bit the dust on Billy Buck, belonging to Flying Five Rodeos; Bruce Ford got a no-score on Beutler & Son's Spooks; Ike Sankey met his match on Franklin's Happy Days; Sam Perkins goose-egged on Joe Kelsey's Last Chance; and Glen Ford was injured severely enough to miss the next three go-arounds and got a no-score in the fifth go on Mesquite's Dare Devil. In all, seven out of fifteen failed to score, and six out of those seven were now out of the running for the average; only Joe Alexander would earn enough points in the other nine go's to end up placing in the average, finishing in the sixth slot.

Chris's sixty-eight was looking better all the time. By the end of the fifth go-around, here's how things looked for the

Gold Buckle: Rusty Riddle had 369 total points to lead the average, followed by Mickey Young with 366, Jack Ward at 359, and Chris LeDoux with 354 points. In the contest for the most money won, which would decide the World Championship, Chris was sitting even better, having the third highest figure at $1,754.17. Riddle and Young were both tied for the top money at $2,192.71.

The sixth go-around was another mediocre draw for Chris, riding a horse called Black Death, from the Rocky Mountain string. He did the best he could on the horse but only ended up with a score of sixty-five. Chick Elms won the round with a seventy-nine.

Chris finally got back into the money in the seventh go-around when he drew a top-notch horse named Sandhills, from Beutler & Sons. Sandhills was a big brown horse with a reputation for being incredibly strong. He pretty much bucked straight across the arena, with a few ducks and swoops, but his strength was so awesome that when Chris finally reached the ground, he noticed the tape on his riding arm had been torn in two. He marked up seventy-three points and won second place behind Royce Smith, who had scored a seventy-five on Mr. Smith, from the Christensen Brothers string. The finish put Chris out in front in the total money earned in the barebacks.

At the NFR, as well as at many other top rodeos across the country, the committee likes to showcase its event leaders, either after an event or prior to a go-around. The NFR uses the start of the following rodeo to put its current leaders on display, and due to Chris's finish in the seventh round, he was required to ride during grand entry in the eighth round.

He was given a pretty little gray horse to ride out into the arena. The grand entry was bothersome for any bareback rider, but for Chris, with his yards of athletic tape, waving to the crowd was something he really didn't need at all! But this was the Finals, and rules were rules, so he relented and made the grand entry run. He would have to repeat the performance the following night as well, before Chick Elms finally edged him out in total money.

In the eighth round, Chris drew a horse called Calamity Jane, from Tommy Steiner's herd. Jane was ordinarily a good draw, as she liked to make a tight circle to the right, giving a cowboy a chance to work for his points. But in this round she was placed in the end chute, and when the gate was opened, she couldn't turn back to the right, since she was already next to the fence; instead, she went straight down the arena with no turn back. As a result, Chris only scored a sixty-eight and finished out of the money in fifth place. Chick Elms won the round with a score of seventy-six on Alsbaugh & Honeycut's Bad Medicine. Chick would also place second the following night, putting him out in front in the overall money for the Finals.

Chris tried hard not to let it show, but he was beginning to get discouraged with the horses it was his misfortune to draw. He knew he needed a good, high jump-kicker on which he could make a good score to bolster his standings. His luck at the draw, however, was not to change.

In the ninth round, he drew Knothead, the same horse that had thrown Joe Alexander in the fifth round. In this round, however, the horse just did a jump-kick crow-hop through the arena, with a long, lunging gait which covered a lot of ground with each stride. The judges weren't impressed, and Chris only scored a sixty-five. Bruce Ford won the round with a score of eighty-two, earned atop Yellow Fever.

At the end of the ninth round, here's the way the competition stood: for the average, Jack Ward (638), Chick Elms (633), Royce Smith (632), Chris LeDoux (625), Rusty Riddle (622), Sandy Kirby (621), and Mickey Young (598); for the most money, and the World Championship, Chick Elms ($3,215.98), Chris LeDoux ($2,631.25), Royce Smith ($2,485.07), Mickey Young and Rusty Riddle ($2,046.52 each), and Sandy Kirby ($1,461.80).

Being thirteen points back, Chris knew it would be difficult to win the average, no matter what he did, but he was in exceptionally good shape in the total money. He knew if he placed high enough in the go-around and did anything at all in the average, he'd have a good shot at it. Chick Elms was the only wild card in the deck, since he alone was ahead of Chris, and could win the Gold Buckle simply by staying within $584 and not letting anyone else pass him up.

The night before the last go-around, the draw was posted, as usual, in the lobby of the Holiday Inn. Normally it was midnight, or later, before the sheets were pinned to the bulletin board, so Chris decided to go back to his room and soak in a nice, hot bath for a while. As he soaked, he ran over the stock pen in his mind, deciding on which animals he'd like to draw and which he'd rather not draw. Moon Rocket was his top choice, with St. Marie (the horse that had broken J.C. Trujillo's hand) and Stormy Weather (the horse that had violently slammed Bruce Ford into the dirt earlier) the bottom choices. The more he thought about Moon Rocket, the more he became convinced that the horse would be his draw. He pictured the moves the horse would make and knew he could win it all on that animal.

When he was finished, he headed back across the parking lot toward the lobby. The draw had already been posted, and several groups of cowboys, having already checked the list, were returning to their rooms for the nght. Chris saw Mickey Young and Bruce Ford walking out of the lobby door, still a few hundred feet away from himself. Mickey looked up, saw Chris, and hollered something that, to Chris, sounded like, "You've got Moon Rocket."

Chris shook his head in disbelief. That was exactly the horse he'd wanted . . . but he wasn't sure he'd heard correctly, so he shouted back, "What did you say?"

"You got Moon Weather," Chris thought he heard him say this time. Now he knew he hadn't heard right, since there was no Moon Weather in the pen.

"What?" Chris demanded again, since the distance between them now was considerably shorter.

"You've got Stormy Weather," Mickey said plainly. Chris's heart stopped. Stormy Weather was probably the strongest horse in the pen. Not one to be easily discouraged, Chris immediately began to bolster his own confidence.

"Well, I'm pretty darned strong, too," he said to himself.

He tossed and turned all night. He had only to think of the horse and the next thing he knew his heart would be pumping and the adrenalin coursing through his veins. Several times he got up, had a chew and paced the floor nervously, trying to make himself drowsy. Finally, at about 4:00 a.m, he drifted off into a light sleep.

The next day, before the rodeo, Chris ran into Bob Tallman, the rodeo announcer, at the hotel coffee shop. Bob said hello and shook his hand.

"Chris," he said, "I'm bettin' on you ... I think you're gonna win it."

Chris smiled and thanked the man, but he tried to let the remark pass. He had been closer than this before and blown it, so he knew not to start polishing that buckle until the stock was all turned out. He went about his pre-rodeo preparations as if it were just another day.

In the afternoon, he climbed into Rosie and motored out towards the coliseum. It was still several hours before the rodeo started, so Chris wasn't in any particular hurry. In the silence of the cab, he considered all the miles he'd put on Rodeo Rose since that first year with Peggy. He remembered their first rodeo together in Bismarck, North Dakota. He remembered the time they had hit a deer near Balmora, Texas, and it had fed them for a week. He thought of San Antonio, Houston, and many other rodeos they had spent together. The truck had become more than just a vehicle; it was a traveling companion and a partner in many fond memories. He felt, after all those thousands of miles, it was only fitting for Rosie to carry him the last five miles to the coliseum, the trip that could earn him the World Championship.

The dressing room was unusually quiet, with everyone deeply involved in their own mental and physical preparations. Royce Smith, who was always the first to arrive, was already spurred-up and smoking a cigarette. Jack Ward and J.C. Trujillio were joking around off to one side, and several others were still on their way from the hotel. Chris took his time, not wanting to get ready too soon and then have too much time to kill.

He sipped a cup of coffee and checked the clock every few minutes. He went over to a group of cowboys and joined in some of their joking and story-telling, trying to relieve some of the pressure beginning to build.

Deciding it was nearly time to get ready, Chris slipped on his tail pad, then carefully began taping his knee. All the while, the tension was twisting him around inside.

"What time is it?" he snapped at Rusty Riddle.

Rusty grinned at him, knowing what was going through his mind and the reason the demand had sounded so harsh. "Seven-thirty," he replied.

Chris strapped on his spurs and ankle straps and began taping his elbow and wrist. Then he put on the shoulder harness and rosined his glove and rigging. In his mind he was going over, again and again, his strategy for the ride.

"I'm gonna try to spur this horse's head off. If I don't, he's gonna splatter me all over the arena," he said to himself.

Next he began stretching and pulling some of the sore, stiff muscles back into shape. He practiced dragging his spurs, one at a time, up the inside of his leg, to just above the knee, firing them back down again, then switching legs.

Finally, the horses were in the chutes and the grand entry was going out. Somehow Chris's horse seemed even bigger than he had before, when he had watched him in the back pen. Chick Elms, who had had to ride in the grand entry, came flying over the fence, and Chris nodded to him and wished him luck. Chris would be out behind Mickey Young.

"Be kinda easy with him," Chris heard someone say from behind him. He turned to see Bobby Steiner, the horse's owner. "He might fight in the chute." Chris smiled at him, then turned back to the horse. A bead of sweat trickled into his eye as he expertly slipped the rigging into place.

Chris looked into the arena to see the first rider make his bid for the purse, and about the same time the chute boss walked down the line, telling the other cowboys to "Pull 'em down."

Chris eased down onto the nervous animal and began working the slack out of the latigos. He reached up and freed the mane from under the front of the rigging, rocking it slightly forward, then back again. As he pulled the rigging tighter and tighter, he wondered just how tight he should go with this horse. He remembered the left turn it had made that sent Ford crashing into the dirt and knew he'd better not let his rigging slip at that point in his own ride. He pulled up just a little bit more on the latigo.

In the chute ahead of him, Mickey Young nodded his face, and Spark Plug, Alsbaugh's former Bareback of the Year, ducked into the arena. Mickey rode him well and was awarded seventy-five points.

"Shoot," Chris said to himself, realizing the ride he would have to make in order to win it.

"All right, Chris," said Bobby, watching Spark Plug exit the arena. "Give it to him."

Chris thought it was nice of Bobby to wish him luck, but he knew deep down inside Bobby really hoped the horse would buck Chris off and win the Bucking Horse of the Year award.

He slid up into his rigging and cracked his hand back into the handhold. One last time, he reminded himself to try to cut the horse's head off, took a deep breath, and nodded his head.

Stormy Weather fired out of the chute high and hard, but Chris had a solid grip with his spurs. With the second jump, he dragged his feet up the neck and pulled hard on the rig ging. The horse was really bucking and blowing, giving Chris the chance he'd been waiting for to really cut loose with everything he had. He knew this was the last horse, and if he hurt himself this time out, he'd have the rest of the winter to heal up, so he just gassed it. One jump at a time, he dragged his spurs up the neck, then fired them back down again to get a hold.

Stormy Weather began angling to the left, then faded to the right. Suddenly, with the force of a freight train, he exploded back to the left, covering at least ten feet sidways. Chris knew instantly that this was the same move that had dusted Bruce Ford. Chris heard the rosin screech, but the hand stayed tight in the rigging. He knew he had taken the very worst the animal could dish out, and he'd made it through the storm. The last few jumps the horse weakened just a bit—he'd had enough.

When the whistle blew and the pick-up man lowered him to the ground, Chris heard Bob Tallman call out his score: "The judges say it's worth seventy-eight points," and the crowd cheered loudly.

He was ahead—for the moment—but there were still several more riders left to try for the money, and Chris knew he wasn't home-free. In order for him to win the average, Jack Ward would have to score less than sixty-five, Chick Elms less than seventy, and Royce Smith less than seventy-one. Then he had to hope Sandy Kirby or Rusty Riddle didn't beat him by more than a couple of points.

He pulled off his gear but listened and watched as each rider made his bid. Sam Perkins got a no-score; Ike Sankey scored a seventy-three; Sandy Kirby received a seventy-six; Rusty Riddle got a sixty-five; T.J. Walter and Jimmy Dix both failed to make a score. Then Royce Smith got a goose-egg. The mighty Joe Alexander mounted Slick Rock and walked away with eighty-two points to take over the lead in the go-around. Chris slipped into second, Sandy Kirby held down third, and Mickey Young was still in fourth.

Chris held his breath when Jack Ward nodded his head. He knew this would be the key to the average; Chris had to beat Jack by thirteen points. It was not to be, though, as Jack scored a respectable seventy-two points. Jack was out of the money for the last go-around but guaranteed first place in the average. The Finals Buckle would go home with Jack.

Jack's money was still below Chris's total, and LeDoux was still in the lead for the World Title. There was only one person who could take that away from him now: Chick Elms.

Chick needed only a score of seventy-six or more to clinch the World Title. He came out and gave it his best shot, but the horse failed to perform to the judges' satisfaction, and they awarded him a re-ride. The tension continued to mount, as Chick went to the re-ride pen.

Chris already knew the re-ride pen contained St. Marie, a rank horse; Three-Bars, one of the all-time great bucking horses; and Moon Rocket, the horse Chris had hoped to draw for himself.

Chick's luck held out—he drew Moon Rocket. The re-ride would be run in during the saddlebronc riding. Chris tried not to think about the importance of this last ride, but there was no escaping it. In a few minutes, the World Championship would be decided.

Moon Rocket was a tough old horse that had made many a cowboy into a champion, as well as serving up some "humble pie" to few old veterans. Earlier in the NFR, this horse had bucked off Glen Ford. Chris knew if Chick rode the horse at all, he would most likely get his seventy-six points.

Chick finally got screwed down for the ride and slid up onto his rigging. As Chris watched from behind the chutes, he felt something wasn't quite right. He couldn't exactly put his finger on it, but Chick called for the gate, and the horse turned out into the arena.

Moon Rocket jumped and kicked high, tilting the cowboy slightly ahead. He jumped and kicked once again, and then dropped his shoulders down hard. Chick's hand was jerked loose, and in just a few more jumps, the rider went sailing over the front end of the horse—to land on his feet. Chris just stared into the arena in a daze. Someone slapped him out of his stupor with a firm slap on the back. "Congratulations, Champ!"

He'd won the World Title.

After all of those years and miles, after the injuries and disappointments, the good times and the bad, his dream had finally come true. Still somewhat dazed, he went out into the coliseum to find a phone. He dialed the number just as the bull riding was beginning.

"Hello?" Peggy answered.

"Hello," said Chris, as a big lump came into his throat. He was trying hard to form the words, realizing the woman on the other end of that phone was a big part of what he had done that night. She had stood by him through all of the hard times, nursed his wounds, acted as trainer and friend, and now she was a major factor in his winning the title. Tears welled up in his eyes, and silence connected them over the phone.

"Chris?" she asked hesitantly.

"I won it," he choked out.

"What?" she exclaimed excitedly, not believing what she had just heard. Just then Don Gay made a great ride, and the coliseum came to life with screaming fans. Chris shouted over the din, "I'm the Champ!"

They both wept and laughed, and suddenly they weren't a thousand miles apart any longer. The dream they had shared for so many years had finally come true, a dream that had lived within him since that windswept day in Cheyenne, so many years ago, when he had performed for a crowd of prairie dogs. Tonight, he had performed for real for over ten-thousand screaming fans and had walked away a winner. Together, they had fulfilled his "Gold Buckle Dream."

The Greatest Prize

I rodeoed on the circuit for nearly fifteen years,
To reach the top, it took a lot of blood, sweat and tears.
I finally won the title, I finally gained the fame,
But, Honey, it don't matter if the whole world knows my
    name.

You stuck by me through thick and thin, just why, Lord only
    knows.
You came along when I sang my songs at all those country
    shows.
And when the lights were shining on me, and me alone,
You stood back in the shadows ... but I want you to know.

Of all the things I've ever done,
I have to tell you true,
The greatest prize I've ever won
Is the love I won from you.

Chris LeDoux (Wyoming Brand Music),
from **Thirty Dollar Cowboy**

Epilogue

I Can't Ride the Broncos Anymore

Well, a man can't spend his life in reflection
Just thinkin' about the way things used to be.
So I'm gonna take myself a new direction,
And make myself some brand new memories.

I spent a lot of years out on the highway
Ridin' buckin' horses for my grub.
But now I make my living with this old guitar,
And just like rodeo, it's in my blood.

I'd make you a wager that I've been in your hometown,
Spurring broncs at your big rodeo.
Now the only time you'll ever see this cowboy come around
Is if I'm singing in a country music show.

Now I'm gonna sing my cowboy music,
With a country feel, and a little touch of soul.
I hope you people take a liking to it,
Yes I do, 'cause I can't ride the broncos anymore.
My body's gettin' too danged tired and sore,
And there's a lotta parts on me that don't work no more.

Chris LeDoux (Wyoming Brand Music),
from **Melodies and Memories**

After winning the World Title, Chris continued to be
plagued by injuries. And to further add to his difficulties, his

little family was beginning to grow rapidly. Since Chris would always place the needs and concerns of his family ahead of his ambitions in rodeo, after a few more years of "going hard," he slipped more into music and ranching for his livelihood.

Chris and Peggy now have five children and ranch on a little place near Kaycee, Wyoming. They have outgrown the small cabin Chris finally finished, which still stands as a testimony to his determination and patience.

After winning a second title became an impossibility, Chris still had a terrible "cravin' to get on 'em," and went to most of the big shows: Calgary, Cheyenne, Houston and some of the others. But soon they, too, were a memory.

Chris's injuries included the bad knee and shoulder which had pained him in 1975, and to these he added his other knee, a severely hyperextended elbow and an enlarged forearm bone that would make the medical books.

But as his rodeo life wound down, his music life was able to blossom with the time to devote to it. Up to this time, Chris had recorded six albums, and his reputation as a fine writer and singer was firmly established. Five of his singles had charted on *Billboard* magazine, reaching into the top one hundred records being played by radio stations.

A German record company had picked up on his music and started to release his albums over there. Later, Chris would twice travel to Germany to appear on their biggest television shows.

He had also established a foothold in Great Britain. Currently, at least twenty-three radio stations in Scotland, England, Ireland and Wales are enthusiastically playing his albums.

Australia and New Zealand added his special songs to their playlists. All of these countries recognize Chris as a true American cowboy, not the "urban" variety. A company in Denmark discovered Chris, and thought so much of him they released an album with Dolly Parton on one side and Chris on the other.

American servicemen also aided in taking Chris and his rodeo songs around the world. To them, his music about the American West was a bit of home away from home.

As many as four hundred American radio stations at a time play cuts from a Chris LeDoux album; these range from Maine to California and up into Alaska, and even include New York City. One of his singles, "Used To Want To Be a Cowboy," went to number twelve in Boston.

Country Joe Flint of KSOP Radio in Salt Lake City states that Chris is probably their most requested artist. He has co-starred in that city in concerts with Don Williams, George Strait, Bobby Bare, Ernest Tubb, and many others.

In 1976, the year he won the World Title in the barebacks, he appeared on national television on the "Challenge of the Sexes." He has appeared on several country music T.V. shows, and was a special guest on two of Nashville's Fan Fair productions.

Over the years, Chris's music has centered on the American West: rodeo, ranch life, livestock, Western folklore, and the like. He has pointedly stayed away from the typical country "bedroom, barroom and cheating" songs, preferring a more "family" appeal.

He has no quarrel with the Nashville music scene, it's just that he'd rather do things his own way—and tens of thousands of loyal fans seem to agree, since his record sales have long since passed the two-million-dollar mark.

Chris now has his own band, "Saddle Boogie," based in Salt Lake City. Rodeo travel got to be very tiring, and at first he was not interested in swapping his spurs for a guitar and staying on the road. But time has passed, his ranch work is caught up, and he's ready to get "On the Road Again."

Look for him in your hometown soon.

Song Acknowledgments

Permission was granted to quote from the following:

THE WINNER—Gary McMahan, Yodeling Yahoo Music

SO YOU WANT TO BE A COWBOY—Chris LeDoux, Wyoming Brand Music

A COWBOY'S GOT TO RIDE—Chris LeDoux, Wyoming Brand Music

BORN TO FOLLOW RODEO—Chris LeDoux, Wyoming Brand Music

HE RIDES THE WILD HORSES—Chris LeDoux, Wyoming Brand Music

BAREBACK JACK—Chris LeDoux, Wyoming Brand Music

JUST RIDING THROUGH—Don Cusic, Blackwood Music

REAL LIVE BUCKEROO—Gary McMahan, Yodeling Yahoo Music

GOIN' AND A-BLOWIN'—Chris LeDoux, Wyoming Brand Music

NATIONAL FINALS—Chris LeDoux, Wyoming Brand Music

TIGHT LEVIS AND YELLOW RIBBONS—Glenn Sutton/ Red Steagall, Talo Duro & Rodeo Cowboy Music

THE COWBOY AND THE HIPPIE—Chris LeDoux, Wyoming Brand Music

OUR FIRST YEAR—Chris LeDoux, Wyoming Brand Music

PHOTO FINISH—Chris LeDoux, Wyoming Brand Music

HE'S A TRYER—Billy Bob Shane, Wyoming Brand Music

IT AIN'T THE YEARS—Chris LeDoux, Wyoming Brand Music

I CAN'T RIDE THE BRONCOS ANY MORE—Chris LeDoux, Wyoming Brand Music

THE GREATEST PRIZE—Chris LeDoux, Wyoming Brand Music